In an age when modern devotionals have been published at an exponential rate, untold riches still lie untapped in the commentary, sermons, and devotional writing of our great forebears. This work makes some of the most spiritually penetrating material of the past accessible to readers today. Don't miss this!

Timothy Keller, *Redeemer Presbyterian Church, New York City*

Imagine bringing the great Reformers to your house for family or personal devotions. This book comes closest to that. Meditate on God's word through these teachers, in simple and succinct but richly profound excerpts, and fresh wind will fill your sails.

Michael Horton, *J. G. Machen Professor of Systematic Theology and Apologetics,*
Westminster Seminary, California

The Protestant Reformers were primarily Bible scholars who wanted the sacred text to transform the church of their day through their preaching and teaching of it. Much of what they said remains relevant to us today, and there is no better way to celebrate their legacy than by sharing in the spiritual impetus that gave their work such great and enduring power.

Gerald Bray, *Research Professor of Divinity, History and Doctrine,*
Beeson Divinity School, Samford University

There is a freshness and power to the words of these Reformers as they share their knowledge of the word of God with us. This book will be a blessing to you as you spend time in the company of these men of God.

Peter Jensen, *Former Anglican Archbishop of Sydney*

I'd love to say that I regularly read the writings of the Reformers but it wouldn't be true. This *Explore by the Book*, however, has the power to change that for me and many others, as Lee Gatiss presents readers with 90 days' worth of pearls from the writings of key Reformers that help us to grasp and cherish and apply truths from God's word.

Nancy Guthrie, *Bible teacher and author of the "Seeing Jesus in the Old Testament"*
Bible-study series

If there was an easy way each day to get some food from the Bible, some gold from the Reformers, some hooks to my brain, and some light for my prayers, I'd be very grateful. I am now very grateful.

Simon Manchester, *Senior Minister, St Thomas' North Sydney,*
and author of "Six Steps to Talking about Jesus"

When I need help understanding the Bible, I turn to the Reformers. Their interpretations are relentlessly faithful, their insights are profoundly pastoral, and their theology is unfailingly biblical. For those reasons, don't miss this fantastic opportunity to read the Bible with Calvin, Luther, Bullinger and Cranmer. With the Holy Spirit's help, you will certainly walk away in awe of God and his gospel.

Matthew Barrett, *Tutor of Systematic Theology and Church History,*
Oak Hill Theological College

Here is a devotional every Christian will find helpful for their walk with Christ. In an accessible and understandable way, the riches of the Scriptures are laid open by some of the great stalwarts of church history. Though belonging to a previous generation, the words of Luther, Calvin, Bullinger and Cranmer will challenge, stir and encourage as they expose the text and the soul of the reader.

Jason Helopoulos, *Associate Pastor, University Reformed Church, and author of*
"A Neglected Grace: Family Worship in the Christian Home"

Contents

EXPLORE BY THE BOOK
Genesis, Exodus, Psalms, Galatians

© The Good Book Company, 2017

Published by:
The Good Book Company

Tel (US): 866 244 2165
Tel (UK): 0333 123 0880
Email (US): info@thegoodbook.com
Email (UK): info@thegoodbook.co.uk

Websites:

North America: www.thegoodbook.com
UK: www.thegoodbook.co.uk
Australia: www.thegoodbook.com.au
New Zealand: www.thegoodbook.co.nz

Unless indicated, all Scripture references are taken from the HOLY BIBLE, NEW INTERNATIONAL VERSION. Copyright © 2011 Biblica, Inc.™ Used by permission.

The Apostles' Creed (page 139) copyright © 1994 Church Society. Used by permission.

ISBN: 9781784980863

Printed in Denmark

Design by André Parker

Introduction

"The words of the LORD are flawless, like silver
purified in a crucible, like gold refined seven times."
(Psalm 12 v 6)

This book is not an end in itself. It is a means of accessing the treasures of a far greater book. Its words are valuable only to the extent that they help you to enjoy the infinite value of words that are perfectly true, gloriously beautiful and utterly wonderful—the words of the LORD.

It is a magnificent thing, in a world which is used to mistakes, to deceit and to confusion, to be able to read flawless, pure, refined words. And that is what you do each time you open your Bible. God does not make errors in anything he says. He does not obscure the truth, by accident or by design. He does not fail to do anything he has said he will do.

That is why this devotional is an "open Bible devotional"—that is, you will need to keep your Bible open, on your lap or on your screen, as you use these studies. You'll be asked questions that bring you to examine and think hard about the text. The aim of the authors is to cause you to spend more time thinking about God's words than their words.

So, rather than seeing these devotionals as snacks, view them as meals. Set aside half an hour in your day to work through the study, and to respond to what you have seen. They are best done daily—but the most crucial thing is for you to find a pattern that is sustainable—better five studies a week for life than seven studies a week for only a week!

Further, since every word of the Lord is flawless, we need to read every word in the Scriptures, rather than sticking to our favourite passages, or to an author's favourites. So *Explore by the Book* works, verse by verse, through whole books or large sections of the Bible. You will be moving through both famous books and not-so-popular ones, and within each book through much-used passages and less-travelled parts. Expect to discover new favourite passages and memory verses that you had never read or noticed or appreciated before!

At the same time, God's word is not always easy to understand. Whether we are completely new to reading it, or have mined its riches many times, all of us still experience "huh?" moments as we struggle to grasp its meaning! So in this devotional series, some of the greatest Bible teachers in the evangelical world help you to dig up the Bible's treasures, and explain their more opaque aspects. They will show you how what you are reading fits into the great overall story of the Scriptures, and will prompt you to apply what you have read to your life.

God's word is not simply pure—it is also purifying. It is the way his Spirit works in his people to challenge and change us. It is designed to move us to worship him with our lips, in our hearts and through our lives. Each day, you will see both of these headings: *Apply* and *Pray*. Use these sections to turn what you have read in God's word into words to speak back to God, and into ways in which you will change your life in response to God.

At the end of each study you'll find a journalling page, for you to record your response to what you have read, either in words or in drawings. Use these pages as you are led to—we all have different ways of making sure we remember what we have seen in the Scriptures, and of responding to those Scriptures. But here are a couple of very straightforward suggestions that you might like to try:

Before you work through the study, read the passage and record...

The Highlight: the truth about God that has most struck you.

The Query: the questions you have about what you have read (and your best attempt at answering them).

The Change: the major way you feel the Spirit is prompting you to change either your attitudes, or your actions, as a result of what you have read.

After you have done the study, record:

One sentence summing up how God has spoken to you through his word.

A short prayer in response to what you have seen.

I hope you enjoy these 90 days listening to the flawless words of the LORD. Be sure that they will excite, change, challenge and comfort you. Be praying that God would use his word to bless you. There is literally nothing like the words of the LORD.

Carl Laferton, Editorial Director
The Good Book Company

Note: This devotional is based on the NIV2011 Bible translation, but it will also work well with either ESV or NIV1984 translations.

Meet the Authors

MARTIN LUTHER (1483-1546) kickstarted the Protestant Reformation by posting his *Ninety-five Theses* against the Roman Catholic practice of indulgences on the door of the Castle Church in Wittenberg on 31st October, 1517. Or so the story goes. A German monk turned university lecturer, Luther had a fiery personality and a penetrating intellect, and his refusal to retract his early writings led to his excommunication by the Pope in 1521. He translated the Bible into vernacular German, and continued to teach theology at Wittenberg until he died in his home town of Eisleben in 1546. His complete works run to 121 volumes, spanning about 80,000 pages.

Featured here are extracts from Luther's commentary on Galatians, transcribed from his lectures given in 1531 and first published in Latin in 1535. The text is taken from the 1575 English translation, which I have freely modernised and updated. "The Epistle to the Galatians is my epistle," Luther once said. "I am betrothed to it. It is my Katie von Bora." Since he compared it to his beloved wife, it is safe to say that he felt a special affinity for Galatians, and this commentary contains many of his key Reformation insights.

JOHN CALVIN (1509-1564) was born in the French town of Noyon, and educated at the University of Paris. He fled France in 1535 and eventually settled in Geneva, having become a Protestant. "I was determined to study in privacy in some obscure place," he wrote in his commentary on the Psalms some years later. But William Farel eventually persuaded him to stay and help him reform the church in Geneva. Calvin reports him saying, "that God would surely curse my peace if I held back from giving help at a time of such great need."

His most famous work is his *Institutes of the Christian Religion*, a highly influential book of systematic theology which he revised and enlarged several times between 1536 and 1559. But also he was a prolific preacher, wrote commentaries on almost all the books of the Bible, founded an academy for the training of pastors and church planters, and reformed the church government and liturgy of Geneva.

Many of Calvin's works were translated into English during his lifetime. The extracts from his commentaries on Genesis and the Psalms featured here are edited and adapted from the nineteenth-century translations by John King and James Anderson in the 22-volume edition of Calvin's commentaries.

HEINRICH BULLINGER (1504-1575) was a Swiss Reformer and pastor of the Grossmünster in Zurich. Though less famous today than Luther and Calvin, he was one of the most influential figures in the Reformation during the sixteenth century itself. He was the primary author of the Second Helvetic Confession (published in 1566), a prolific letter-writer, and part of a wide network of Protestant Reformers throughout Europe. He also wrote several Bible commentaries and works of theology, many of which were translated into English during his lifetime.

Bullinger's most influential work was his *Decades*—not an outline of church history but a collection of Latin sermons, carefully arranged into five sets of ten (and totalling around 700,000 words!). The extracts here from his sermons on the Apostles' Creed and on the Ten Commandments are updated and modernised from the first English translation, which was published in 1577.

THOMAS CRANMER (1489-1556) was the chief architect of the English Reformation. Educated at the University of Cambridge, Cranmer rose to become Archbishop of Canterbury in 1533. He helped Henry VIII and Thomas Cromwell break England away from Rome, and established the liturgical and doctrinal framework for the newly independent and reformed Church of England. For this (and probably because he helped to build the case against Henry's marriage to her mother), the Roman Catholic Queen Mary had him burnt at the stake in Oxford.

The *First Book of Homilies* was published in 1547, and was intended to ensure that there was good, sound preaching in every Church of England parish each Sunday. Not all ministers were licensed or able to preach their own sermons, and so the Homilies (written by Cranmer and others) were there to make up for this obvious lack. The extracts here (every seventh day) are almost all by Cranmer, with a couple also being taken from the homily on sin first drafted by John Harpsfield (1516-1578), who was educated at New College, Oxford, and was a notable professor of Greek.

Article 35 of *The Thirty-nine Articles of Religion* (still the legal doctrinal basis of the Church of England) states that these official Homilies contain "godly and wholesome doctrine". The great evangelical leader of the 18th century, George Whitefield, said they contain "the grand doctrines of the Reformation". The text here is taken from my updated and modernised edition published by Church Society.

LEE GATISS (a child of the 1970s) has degrees in theology and history from Oxford and Cambridge Universities, Oak Hill College, London, and Westminster Theological Seminary, Philadelphia. Despite that, he's surprisingly normal, has been married to Kerry for more than 20 years, and has three children, two rabbits, and a couple of guinea pigs. He's currently the Director of Church Society, Lecturer in Church History at Union School of Theology, and Research Fellow of the Jonathan Edwards Centre Africa at the University of the Free State, South Africa. He is the author/editor of a number of books on the Bible, theology and church history, including *The Forgotten Cross* and *The NIV Proclamation Bible*. You can also find him at facebook.com/lectionarylee.

Lee has selected, updated and edited the extracts from the Reformers that you will find here, and has written the opening questions, applications and prayer suggestions. There is also a glossary at the back of the book to help explain some of the trickier words and concepts you may come across.

Many of the works of Luther, Calvin, Bullinger, Cranmer, and other Reformers are available for free online at prdl.org and ccel.org.

Sent
by Jesus

Galatians 1 v 1-5

with Martin Luther

We begin our exploration of the Bible with the Protestant Reformers by tucking into the work of Martin Luther on Galatians—"my dear epistle" as he called it.

Read Galatians 1 v 1-5

Why do you think Paul insists so strongly that his ministry is "not from men" (v 1)?

Does Paul mention his status for his own glory or for some other reason, do you think?

Paul's Calling

When Paul so highly commends his calling, he is not seeking his own praise. But with a necessary and a holy pride he magnifies his ministry. That is to say, *I want people to receive me, not as Paul of Tarsus, but as Paul the apostle and ambassador of Jesus Christ.* And he does this to maintain his authority, that the people, in hearing this, might be more attentive and willing to give ear to him.

This is the first assault that Paul makes against the false apostles, who ran when no one sent them. Calling, therefore, is not to be despised. For it is not enough for someone to have the word and pure doctrine, but they must also be assured of their calling. So our fantastical* spirits at this day have the words of faith in their mouths, but yet they yield no fruit, for their chief end and purpose is to draw people to their false and perverse opinions.

*Note: Some unusual or jargon words are explained in the Glossary on page 281.

The Seriousness of Word Ministry

This then is our comfort, that we who are in the ministry of the word have an office which is heavenly and holy. Being lawfully called to this, we triumph against all the gates of hell. We see then how good and necessary Paul's boasting is.

In times past when I was a young theologian and teacher, I thought Paul was unwise to glory so often in his calling in all his epistles. But I did not understand his purpose. For I did not know that the ministry of God's word was so weighty a matter. I knew nothing of the doctrine of faith, because there was then no certainty taught either in the universities or churches, but all was full of the clever subtleties of academics. And therefore no-one was able to understand the dignity and power of this holy and spiritual boasting. True and lawful calling serves, first, to the glory of God and, secondly, to the advancing of our office. Moreover, it also serves to the salvation of ourselves and of the people.

⊙ Apply

Would it be right to think of Paul's letters as "just his opinion" or as simply a record of his experience of the grace of God? If not, why not?

Given that they are not apostles as Paul was, how should we think of those who teach and preach the Bible today? Do you think Luther is right to draw some comparisons between them?

⊙ Pray

Pray that you would listen attentively to Paul's teaching from Galatians, as a gift to us from God.

Pray too for those who preach and teach in your church, that they would know the weightiness of their calling, and do everything for God's glory.

~ Notes and Prayers ~

Day
2

Christic
Gave Himself

Galatians 1 v 1-5

with Martin Luther

Today we look at a verse that Luther said was "a singular comfort to those who are terrified by the greatness of their sins".

Read Galatians 1 v 1-5 again

What is the link between verses 3 and 4?

Why do you think Paul includes verse 4 in his opening greeting?

Christ Has Given Himself

Paul has nothing in his mouth but Christ, and therefore in every word there is a fervency of spirit and life. Mark how well and to the purpose he speaks. He does not say Christ, "who has *received* our works at our hands", nor "who has received the sacrifices of Moses' Law, worshippings, religions, masses, vows, and pilgrimages".

No. Christ has *given*. What has he given? Not gold nor silver, nor beasts, nor Passover lambs, nor an angel, but himself. For what? Not for a crown; not for a kingdom; not for our holiness or righteousness—but for our sins.

These words are very thunder claps from heaven against all kinds of righteousness. Therefore we must with diligent attention mark Paul's every word, and not slenderly consider them or lightly pass them over. For they are full of consolation, and confirm fearful consciences exceedingly.

Satisfaction for Sin

How may we obtain forgiveness of our sins? Paul answers that the man called Jesus Christ, the Son of God, has given himself for them. These are excellent and most comfortable words—our sins are taken away by no other means than by the Son of God delivered unto death. With such guns and such artillery must the system of our opponents be destroyed, and all the religions of the heathen, all works, all merits and all superstitious ceremonies. For if our sins may be taken away by our own works, merits and satisfactions, why did the Son of God need to be given up for them?

But seeing that he was given for them, it follows that we cannot do away with them by our own works. Again, by this sentence it is declared that our sins are so great, so infinite and invincible, that it is impossible for the whole world to satisfy for one of them. And surely the greatness of the ransom (namely Christ, the Son of God, who gave himself for our sins) declares sufficiently that we can neither satisfy for sin, nor have dominion over it.

⊙ Apply

Is it a comfort to you that, rather than demanding something for your sins, Christ gave himself for them? If not, why not?

How awful must our sins be that the only remedy for them was for Christ, the Son of God, to give himself up to death for them? Do you think of your sins in this way?

⊙ Pray

Praise God for his grace towards us in sending Jesus to die in our place on the cross.

Thank Jesus for rescuing us from the present evil age, which has been ruined by sin and is under God's curse.

~ Notes and Prayers ~

Day

3

Falling Away Is Easy

Galatians 1 v 6-10

with Martin Luther

Congregations which are won by great labour may easily and quickly be overthrown, so we ought carefully to watch out for the devil, lest he sneaks in while we sleep.

Read Galatians 1 v 6-10

How did Paul feel about the churches he had planted deserting the gospel?

How had this happened?

Overturning the Gospel

See how Paul complains that to fall and to err in the faith is an easy matter. A minister may labour ten years to get some little church to be rightly and religiously ordered; and when it is so ordered, there creeps in some mad, unlearned idiot, who knows nothing but how to speak slanderously against the sincere preachers of the word, and they in one moment overthrow all.

We by the grace of God have gotten here at Wittenberg the form of a Christian church. The word is purely taught among us, the sacraments are rightly used, and all things go forward prosperously. This most happy course of the gospel some mad head would soon stop, and in one moment would overturn all that we in many years have built with great labour.

This happened even to Paul, the elect vessel of Christ. He had won the churches of Galatia with great care, but in a short time after his departure the false apostles overthrew them. We so walk in the midst of Satan's snares that one fantastical head may destroy in a short space all that which many true ministers, labouring night and day, have built up.

Caring for the Church

Seeing then that the church is so soft and so tender a thing, and is so soon overthrown, we must watch carefully against these fantastical spirits, who, when they have heard a few sermons or have read a few pages in the holy Scriptures, make themselves masters and controllers of all learners and teachers, contrary to common authority.

At the first, when the light of the gospel began to appear, after such a great darkness of human traditions, many were zealously bent to godliness. They heard sermons greedily and had the ministers of God's word in reverence. But now, when the doctrine of piety and godliness is happily reformed, with so great an increase of God's word, many which before seemed earnest disciples become despisers and very enemies. They not only cast off the study of God's word, and despise its ministers, but also hate all good learning.

⊙ Apply

First, we must watch ourselves. Are you still zealous for the true gospel message and keen to pass it on faithfully?

Second, what can you do to help ensure that your church does not turn away to a different gospel?

⊙ Pray

Pray for your own heart to remain faithful to the true gospel.

Pray that false teaching does not enter your church; and that if it does, it is driven away by faithful ministers.

~ Notes and Prayers ~

_____

_____

_____

_____

_____

_____

_____

_____

_____

_____

_____

_____

_____

_____

_____

_____

_____

_____

_____

_____

_____

_____

Day

4

To the Glory of God Alone

Galatians 1 v 11-24

with Martin Luther

Don't believe Luther, or the church, or the fathers, or the apostles—not even an angel from heaven—if they teach anything against the revealed word of God.

Read Galatians 1 v 11-24

Where did Paul's gospel come from (v 11-12)?

Why do you think Paul talks about the journeys he made after his conversion?

The Gospel Came from God

Paul says he did not learn his gospel from any man, but received it by a revelation. But the matter of justification is fickle—not of itself (for of itself it is most sure and certain)—but in respect of us. I myself have good experience of this. For I know in what hours of darkness I sometimes wrestle. I know how often suddenly I lose the beams of the gospel and grace, as being shadowed from me with thick and dark clouds.

I know in what a slippery place others who seem to have sure footing in matters of faith also do stand. In respect of us, it is a very fickle matter, because we are fickle. Therefore we teach continually that the knowledge of Christ and of faith is no work of man, but simply the gift of God. As he creates faith, so does he keep it in us.

Giving All Glory to God

I attribute all things to God alone, and nothing to man. When I first took upon me the defence of the gospel, I remember that a worthy man said to me, "I really like that this doctrine which you preach yields all glory to God alone, and nothing to man: for to God there cannot be attributed too much glory, goodness, and mercy". This saying greatly comforted and confirmed me. And it is true that the doctrine of the gospel takes from men all glory, wisdom and righteousness, and gives them to the Creator alone.

It is much safer to attribute too much to God than to man. For in this case I may say boldly: Even if the church, Augustine and other doctors, Peter and Apollos— yes, even an angel from heaven—teach a contrary doctrine, yet my doctrine is such, that it sets forth and preaches the grace and glory of God alone. And in the matter of salvation, it condemns the righteousness and wisdom of all. In this case I cannot offend, because I give both to God and man that which properly and truly belongs to them both.

⊘ Apply

Does your confidence as a Christian come from the gospel revelation itself or from some other source (such as your church, your pastor, your knowledge, your credentials)?

When church people let you down, or you struggle to believe, do you turn back to the revelation of God in the Bible, or to something else?

⊙ Pray

Thank God that the good news of Jesus has been proclaimed to you, and that he gave you faith to believe it.

Ask God to help you continue trusting in his gospel rather than in any merely human authority.

~ Notes and Prayers ~

_____

_____

_____

_____

_____

_____

_____

_____

_____

_____

_____

_____

_____

_____

_____

_____

_____

_____

_____

_____

_____

Day

5

By Faith Alone

Galatians 2 v 1-10

with Martin Luther

W e should not allow our consciences to be bound to any "work", so that by doing this thing or that we consider ourselves righteous, or by leaving it undone we think we are damned.

Read Galatians 2 v 1-10

Why was it so important to Paul that Titus was not forced to be circumcised (v 3-5)?

What liberating truth of the gospel was Paul trying to defend against the "you must be circumcised" group (v 5)?

The Place of Circumcision

Paul did not reject circumcision as a damnable thing. Neither did he, by word or deed, force the Jews to forsake it. But he rejected circumcision as a thing not necessary to righteousness. The Old Testament patriarchs themselves were not justified by circumcision, but for them it was only a sign or a seal of righteousness by which they showed and exercised their faith.

Hearing that circumcision was not necessary for righteousness, the believing Jews who were still weak and had a zeal for the Old Testament Law thought this meant that it was altogether unprofitable and damnable. And the false apostles only encouraged this fond opinion, so that the hearts of the people would be stirred up by this against Paul, and so they might thoroughly discredit his doctrine.

EXPLORE BY THE BOOK

Similarly, we today do not reject fasting and other good exercises as damnable things. But we do teach that by these exercises we do not obtain forgiveness of sins. When the people hear this, they judge us to speak against good works. But for many years past there has been none that has more truly and faithfully taught concerning good works than we do!

Faith Alone

Now the *truth* of the gospel is that our righteousness comes by faith *only*—without the works of the law. The *corruption* of the gospel is that we are justified by faith, but not without also doing the works of the law. With conditions like these, the false apostles also preached their gospel.

Others preach in the same way today. For they say that we must believe in Christ, and that faith is the foundation of our salvation—but it does not justify someone, unless it is also furnished with love. This is not the truth of the gospel, but false-hood and misrepresentation. The true gospel is that works or love are not the ornament or perfection of faith, but that faith itself is God's gift and God's work in our hearts, which therefore justifies us because it takes hold of Christ our redeemer.

⊙ Apply

Is there any good work or good cause that people say (or imply) you have to embrace to be a "proper Christian"? Is it right to add that as a requirement to "faith alone"?

Is it just "being picky" to insist that justification is by faith alone?

⊙ Pray

Praise God that through the gospel we are justified by faith alone, which is his gift.

Ask God to help you speak about this issue clearly and defend it.

~ Notes and Prayers ~

_____

_____

_____

_____

_____

_____

_____

_____

_____

_____

_____

_____

_____

_____

_____

_____

_____

_____

_____

_____

_____

_____

Not
by Works

Galatians 2 v 11-21

with Martin Luther

It is a horrible blasphemy to imagine that there is any work by which you could presume to pacify God.

Read Galatians 2 v 11-21

Note: Cephas is another name for Peter.

Why was Peter's behaviour not in line with the gospel (v 14)?

How does Paul describe the true Christian life in these verses?

True Religion

Paul briefly summarised the principal article of all Christian doctrine, which makes true Christians indeed, when he said, "We [are] justified by faith and not by the works of the law". This our opponents do not believe, but continue to say, "Whoever does this good work or that deserves forgiveness of sins", or "Whoever enters into this or that holy order, and keeps this rule, to him we assuredly promise everlasting life".

But if no flesh is justified by the works of the law, much less shall it be justified by the Rule of Benedict, Francis, or Augustine, in which there is not one jot of true faith in Christ; but this only they urge, that whoever keeps these things has life everlasting.

I have often marvelled how the true church could endure and continue as it has done, since these destructive heresies have reigned for so many years in such great darkness and errors. But there were some whom God called by the letter of the gospel and by baptism. These walked in simplicity and humbleness of heart, thinking that the monks and friars, and such only as were anointed by the bishops, were religious and holy, and they themselves were profane and secular, and not worthy to be compared to them. Therefore, finding in themselves no good works to set against the wrath and judgment of God, they did fly to the death and passion of Christ, and were saved in this simplicity.

Christian Righteousness

But this we may plainly see, that there is nothing here for us *to do*. It belongs to us, rather, only to hear that these things have been *done* for us, and by faith to grasp hold of them.

In verse 20, Paul says, "I no longer live, but Christ lives in me". Here he plainly shows by what means he lives. He teaches what true Christian righteousness is, namely the righteousness by which Christ lives in us, and not that which is in our own person. Christ is my righteousness and life.

⊘ Apply

What do you think a really good Christian life looks like? Would Luther or Paul agree?

What barriers do we put in the way of other Christians, or what hoops do we make them jump through to be truly accepted?

⊘ Pray

Praise "the Son of God, who loved me and gave himself for me" (v 20).

Ask the Lord to show you how to live for God by faith in Jesus, without trusting in your own works or insisting that others do them too.

~ Notes and Prayers ~

Day

7

No Stinking Puddles!

2 Timothy 3 v 10-17

with Thomas Cranmer

Every seventh day we will explore one of the Anglican Homilies, or sermons, written by Thomas Cranmer and others, recognised in the Reformation as containing "wholesome doctrine".

Read 2 Timothy 3 v 10-17

What does Paul say the Bible is?

What does he say the Bible is for?

A Satisfying Fountain

There can be nothing either more necessary or more profitable for a Christian than the knowledge of holy Scripture, since in it is contained God's true word, setting forth both his glory and mankind's duty. And there is no truth nor doctrine necessary for our justification and everlasting salvation, but it is (or may be) drawn out of that fountain and well of truth.

Therefore, as many as are desirous to enter into the right and perfect way to God must apply their minds to know holy Scripture, without which they can neither sufficiently know God and his will, or their office and duty. And as drink is pleasant to them that are dry, and meat to them that are hungry, so is the reading, hearing, searching and studying of holy Scripture to those that are desirous to know God, or themselves, and to do his will.

Unpleasant Truth

However, for those who are so drowned in worldly vanities that they neither savour God nor any godliness, their stomachs loathe and abhor the heavenly knowledge and food of God's word. For that is the cause why they desire such vanities, rather than the true knowledge of God.

When someone is sick with a fever, whatever they eat or drink (though it is never so pleasant), it is as bitter to them as wormwood, not for the bitterness of the meat but for the corrupt and bitter taste that is in their own tongue and mouth. Even so is the sweetness of God's word bitter, not of itself, but only to those who have their minds corrupted by being long accustomed to sin and love of this world.

Therefore, forsaking the corrupt judgment of carnal and worldly people, who care only for their physical carcass, let us reverently hear and read holy Scripture, which is the food of the soul. Let us diligently search for the well of life, in the books of the Old and New Testament, and not run to the stinking puddles of human traditions, devised by human imagination, for our justification and salvation.

⊙ Apply

Do you have a hunger for God's word, or are you "drowned in worldly vanities"?

What "stinking puddles of human traditions" are you tempted to drink from?

⊙ Pray

Thank God for revealing himself and his will to us in the Bible.

Pray for God to give you an appetite for his word, rather than for the pleasures of this world.

~ Notes and Prayers ~

Righteous Sinners

Galatians 3 v 1-9

with Martin Luther

I t is an unspeakable gift that God accepts us as righteous without works, when we embrace his Son by faith alone—even our imperfect faith.

Read Galatians 3 v 1-9

How is the way we begin the Christian life related to the way we continue (v 2-5)?

What do Christian believers have in common with Abraham (v 6-9)?

God Accepts My Imperfect Faith

Let those who study the word of God learn from this saying: "Abraham 'believed God, and it was credited (counted) to him as righteousness'". This sets forth rightly what true Christian righteousness is—a faith and confidence in the Son of God, or rather a confidence of the heart in God through Jesus Christ.

This faith and confidence is accounted righteousness for Christ's sake. For these two things work Christian righteousness: namely, faith in the heart, which is a gift of God and rightly believes in Christ; and also, that God accepts this imperfect faith for perfect righteousness, for the sake of Christ, in whom I have come to believe.

Because of this faith in Christ, God does not see my doubting of his good will to-wards me, my distrust, my heaviness of spirit, and other sins which are yet in me. For as long as I live in the flesh, sin is truly in me. But because I am covered under the shadow of Christ's wings, as is the chicken under the wing of the hen, God covers and pardons the remnant of sin in me. That is to say, because of that faith by which I began to lay hold on Christ, he accepts my imperfect righteousness even for perfect righteousness, and counts my sin for no sin, even though it is sin indeed.

Righteous and Sinful Simultaneously

Thus a Christian is both righteous and a sinner, holy and profane, an enemy of God and yet a child of God. Our opponents cannot accept these paradoxes, for they do not know the true manner of justification. And this is why they make people work hard until they should feel no sin at all in them—and thereby they give occasion to many to become stark mad. Many of them, striving (unsuccessfully) with all their endeavour to be perfectly righteous, at the point of death were driven into desperation. Which would have happened to me also, if Christ had not mercifully looked on me and helped me out of this error.

⊙ Apply

Be comforted by the fact that, when you are a Christian, God accepts even your imperfect and wavering faith and counts it as righteousness.

Rejoice that you can be counted as completely right with God even though you are still a sinner.

⊙ Pray

Pray for any you know who are stuck in the error of thinking they have to be perfectly righteous in themselves in order to be acceptable to God.

Praise and thank God that he covers and forgives your sin, even your distrust, and accepts your imperfect faith.

~ Notes and Prayers ~

_____

_____

_____

_____

_____

_____

_____

_____

_____

_____

_____

_____

_____

_____

_____

_____

_____

_____

_____

_____

_____

_____

_____

_____

Day
9

The Happy Exchange

Galatians 3 v 10-20

with Martin Luther

M aking a happy exchange with us, Christ took upon himself our sinful person, and gave to us his innocent and victorious person.

Read Galatians 3 v 10-20

Why is there a curse on people who rely on the law to save them (v 10-11)?

How did Christ become a curse for us (v 13)?

Punished in My Place

Christ is innocent as concerning his own person, and therefore he ought not to have been hanged upon a cross. But because, according to the Law of Moses, every thief ought to be hanged, therefore Christ also according to the Law ought to be hanged, for he took the person of a sinner and of a thief—not of one, but of all sinners and thieves. For we are sinners and thieves, and therefore guilty of death and everlasting damnation. But Christ took all our sins upon him, and for them died upon the cross.

Christ was not only crucified and died, but sin also (through the divine love) was laid upon him. When sin was laid upon him, then along comes the Law and says, "Every sinner must die. Therefore, O Christ, if you become guilty and suffer punishment for sinners, you must also bear sin and curse."

Because he had taken upon himself our sins, not by constraint, but of his own good will, it was fitting for him to bear the punishment and wrath of God—not for his own person (which was just and invincible, and therefore could in no way be found guilty) but for us.

Not Merely an Example

Some try to rob us of this knowledge of Christ and this most heavenly comfort when they separate him from sins and sinners, and only set him forth to us as an example to be followed. But we must know him to be wrapped in our sins, in our curse, in our death, and in all our evils, just as he is wrapped in our flesh and in our blood.

Let us therefore receive this doctrine, which is most sweet and full of comfort with thanksgiving, and with an assured faith—a faith which teaches that Christ being made a curse for us (that is, a sinner subject to the wrath of God) did put upon him our person, and laid our sins upon his own shoulders, saying, "I have committed the sins which all men have committed".

⊙ Apply

Meditate on the humility and grace of Christ that he stooped so very low, wrapping himself in our flesh and blood so he could wrap himself in our sin and curse.

Ponder how we would have to bear the wrath and curse of God if Jesus had not done it for us.

⊙ Pray

Praise God that Jesus took the punishment for your sins and bore God's wrath in your place.

Thank God for the comfort of having Jesus not just as an example to follow but as a Saviour who put himself in harm's way for us.

~ Notes and Prayers ~

_____

_____

_____

_____

_____

_____

_____

_____

_____

_____

_____

_____

_____

_____

_____

_____

_____

_____

_____

_____

_____

_____

Children of God

Galatians 3 v 21-29

with Martin Luther

The true use of the Old Testament Law is to teach us, so that we are brought to the knowledge of our sin and humbled, that we may come to Christ and be children of God.

Read Galatians 3 v 21-29

What does it mean for the Law to be a guardian or schoolmaster (v 24-25)?

Why is being a child of God such an amazing blessing (v 26-29)?

The Law as Our Schoolmaster

A schoolmaster is appointed to teach children, to bring them up, and to keep them, as it were, in prison. But to what end, or how long? Is it to the end that this sharp dealing of the schoolmaster should always continue? Or that the child should remain in continual bondage? Not so, but only for a time, that this obedience, this prison and correction might turn to the profit of the child, that in time they might be heir and prince.

For it is not a father's will that his child should be always subject to the schoolmaster, and always beaten with rods—but that by this instruction and discipline they may be made fit and able to be the father's successor. Even so the Law (says Paul) is nothing else but a schoolmaster—not for ever, but until it has brought us to Christ.

By this, Paul shows us what the true use of the Law is—namely, that it does not justify hypocrites, for they remain without Christ in their presumption and security; but rather, that it does not leave those who are of a contrite heart in death and damnation, but drives them to Christ.

The Blessing of Adoption

Paul does not say, "You are the children of God because you are circumcised, because you have heard the Law and have done its works" (as the Jews do imagine, and the false apostles teach)—but "by faith in Jesus Christ". The Law then does not make us the children of God, and much less do human traditions.

Faith in Christ makes us the children of God, and not the Law. What tongue either of men or angels can sufficiently extol and magnify the great mercy of God towards us, that we who are miserable sinners and by nature the children of wrath, should be called to this grace and glory? We are made the children and heirs of God, fellow heirs with the Son of God, and lords over heaven and earth, and that only by means of our faith which is in Christ Jesus.

⊘ Apply

Do you appreciate how great a blessing it is to be considered a child of God, by faith alone? How do you show your appreciation?

Does the Law, when it reveals your sin and humbles you, make you turn to Christ for forgiveness, or drive you into despair?

⊙ Pray

Praise God for turning us from children of wrath into children of God, not by imposing on us the weighty Law, but simply by faith in Jesus.

Ask God to give you a contrite heart which humbly rejoices in the blessing of being his child.

~ Notes and Prayers ~

_____

_____

_____

_____

_____

_____

_____

_____

_____

_____

_____

_____

_____

_____

_____

_____

_____

_____

_____

_____

_____

_____

_____

Day

II

The Spirit and the Word

Galatians 4 v 1-11

with Martin Luther

W hen we willingly and gladly hear the word about Christ preached, be assured that God, by and with this preaching, sends the Holy Spirit into our hearts.

Read Galatians 4 v 1-11

What are the benefits of being a child of God?

How does being a child of God affect our relationship to the Law?

Signs of the Spirit

The Holy Spirit is sent by the word into the hearts of believers. This sending is without any visible appearance; rather, by the hearing of the external word, we receive an inward fervency and light—by which we are changed and become new creatures, and receive a new mind, a new feeling, and a new moving. This change is the gift and operation of the Holy Spirit, which comes with the word preached, which purifies our hearts by faith, and brings forth in us spiritual motions.

And although it may not appear to the world that we are renewed in spirit and have the Holy Spirit, yet our speech and our confession do declare sufficiently that the Holy Spirit with his gifts is in us.

We ought not therefore to doubt whether the Holy Spirit dwells in us or not, but to be assuredly persuaded that we are the temple of the Holy Spirit, as Paul says (1 Corinthians 3 v 16; 6 v 19). For if anyone feels in themselves a love towards the word of God, and willingly hears, talks, writes and thinks of Christ, let that person know that this is not the work of human will or reason, but the gift of the Holy Spirit. For it is impossible that these things should be done without the Holy Spirit.

Contempt for the Word

On the other hand, where there is hatred and contempt for the word, there the devil (the god of this world) reigns, blinding people's hearts and holding them captive, that the gospel—the glory of Christ—should not shine on them (2 Corinthians 4 v 4). Which is what we see at this day in the majority of people, who have no love for the word but presumptuously treat it with contempt as though it had nothing at all to do with them.

But whoever feels any love or desire for the word, let them acknowledge with thankfulness that this affection is poured into them by the Holy Spirit. For we are not born with this affection and desire.

⊙ Apply

Does your speech "sufficiently declare" that the Holy Spirit is in you? Why / why not?

Do you love the word of God and willingly hear, talk, and think of Christ?

⊙ Pray

Pray that the Holy Spirit would fan into flame your love for his word.

Pray for those who treat God's word with contempt, including any you know personally, that the Spirit would open the eyes of their hearts to it.

~ Notes and Prayers ~

Patience
and Perplexity

Galatians 4 v 12-20

with Martin Luther

P aul used sweet and gentle words so that if he had offended anyone he might win them back to the truth again by these loving words and fatherly affection.

Read Galatians 4 v 12-20

Why is Paul perplexed about the Galatians (v 20)?

What had changed their attitude towards him (v 17)?

Patient Pastoring

By his own example, Paul admonishes all pastors and ministers, that they ought to have a fatherly and motherly affection—not towards ravening wolves, but towards the poor sheep who are miserably seduced and going astray, patiently bearing with their faults and infirmities, instructing and restoring them with the spirit of meekness. For they cannot be brought into the right way again by any other means. By overly sharp reproving and rebuking they are provoked to anger, or else to desperation, but not to repentance.

Error Creates Disunity

Such is the nature and fruit of true and sound doctrine that when it is well taught and well understood, it joins people's hearts together with a singular concord. But when people reject godly and sincere doctrine, and embrace errors, this unity and concord is soon broken. Therefore as soon as you see your brethren seduced (by vain and fantastical spirits) to fall from the doctrine of justification, you will perceive that by and by they will pursue the faithful with bitter hatred, whom before they most tenderly loved.

This we find to be true at this day in our false brethren and other breakaway groups, who at the beginning of the reformation of the gospel were glad to hear us and read our books with great zeal and affection. They acknowledged the grace of the Holy Spirit in us, and reverenced us for that as the ministers of God. Some of them also lodged with us for a time. But when they departed from us and were perverted by the wicked doctrine of the breakaway groups, they showed themselves more bitter enemies to our doctrine and our name than any other.

I do much and often marvel why they should conceive such a deadly hatred against us, whom they before so dearly and so tenderly loved. Even they are constrained to confess that we desire nothing more than that the glory of God may be advanced and the truth of the gospel purely taught—which God has now again in these latter days revealed by us to this ungrateful world.

⊙ Apply

Why do you think is it hard to be patient and meek with those who seem to be wandering away from the gospel?

How true is it that people who once embraced but then move away from the gospel message Luther is talking about often become bitter enemies of it?

⊙ Pray

Pray that God would give you patience and gentleness in your relationships with those who seem to be wandering from the truth.

Ask God to keep your church faithful to and united in the truth of the gospel.

~ Notes and Prayers ~

Day

13

Persecution

Galatians 4 v 21-31

with Martin Luther

There will always be persecution in the church, especially when the doctrine of the gospel flourishes. The "children of the flesh" mock the "children of the promise".

Read Galatians 4 v 21-31

Why do you think Paul uses an example from Genesis to try and persuade his readers?

Why is it significant that Hagar's child (Ishmael, here in Galatians 4 representing those who seek salvation through works) persecuted Sarah's (Isaac, representing those who trust in God's salvation promises) (v 29)?

Persecution Is Inevitable

This passage contains a singular consolation. Whoever is born and lives in Christ, and rejoices in this birth and inheritance of God, has Ishmael for their enemy and their persecutor. This we learn today by experience: for we see that all the world is full of tumults, persecutions, and breakaway groups. If we did not arm ourselves with this consolation of Paul, and well understand this doctrine of justification, we should never be able to withstand the violence and subtle sleights of Satan.

Truly, it is no small grief to us when we are forced to hear that all things were in peace and tranquillity before the gospel came, and that since the preaching and publishing of it, all things are unquiet and the whole world is in an uproar. When someone who is not endued with the Spirit of God hears this, they are offended and judge that infinite evils do proceed directly from the doctrine of the gospel.

Against this great offence we must comfort and arm ourselves with this sweet consolation, that the faithful must bear this name and this title in the world—that they are troublemakers who promote division, and the authors of innumerable evils. This is why our adversaries think they have a just cause, and even that they do God high service, when they hate, persecute and kill us.

Enduring Persecution

It is inevitable then, that Ishmael must persecute Isaac. But Isaac does not persecute Ishmael. Whoever will not suffer the persecution of Ishmael, let them not profess to be a Christian. Whoever wants to preach Christ truly, and confess him to be our righteousness, must be content to hear that they are a pernicious fellow.

Such tumults and hurly-burlies we hear and see at this day. The adversaries lay the fault in our doctrine. But the doctrine of grace and peace does not stir up these troubles. Moreover, the doctrine for which they raise up such tumults is not ours, but it is the doctrine of Christ. This doctrine we cannot deny, nor give up the defence of it (Luke 9 v 26).

⊙ Apply

What would you say to someone who claimed the Reformation was a huge tragedy because it divided the church?

What would you say to someone who asked, "Why can't Christians all just get along?"

⊖ Pray

Pray for those who face serious and violent persecution for being Christians, that they would stand firm in their faith.

Pray for those who persecute Christians, especially those who are themselves within the church, that God would grant them repentance and a knowledge of the truth.

~ Notes and Prayers ~

_____

_____

_____

_____

_____

_____

_____

_____

_____

_____

_____

_____

_____

_____

_____

_____

_____

_____

_____

_____

_____

_____

Day

14

The Usefulness of Scripture

Psalm 19 v 7-14

with Thomas Cranmer

I n today's extract from the Anglican Homilies, we see why the Bible ought to be much in our hands, in our eyes, in our ears, in our mouths, and in our hearts.

Read Psalm 19 v 7-14

What do the words (laws, precepts, etc.) of the Lord do?

What would we be without the words of God, his commandments and rules?

Knowing God and Ourselves

Holy Scripture fully contains what we ought to do and what to avoid, what to believe, what to love, and what to look for at God's hands at length. In those books we shall find the Father from whom, the Son by whom, and the Holy Spirit in whom all things have their being and conservation; and these three persons are but one God, and one substance.

In these books, we may learn to know ourselves, how vile and miserable we are, and also to know God, how good he is of himself and how he communicates his goodness to us, and to all creatures. We may learn also in these books to know God's will and pleasure, as much as (for this present time) is convenient for us to know. And whatsoever is required for our salvation is fully contained in the Scripture of God.

Something for Everyone

Those who are ignorant may there learn and have knowledge. Those who are hard-hearted, and obstinate sinners, shall there find eternal torments (prepared by God's justice) to make them afraid, and to soften them. Those who are oppressed with misery in this world shall there find relief in the promises of eternal life, to their great consolation and comfort. Those who are wounded (by the devil) to death shall find there medicine, by which they may be restored again to health.

If it is necessary to teach any truth, or reprove false doctrine, to rebuke any vice, to commend any virtue, to give good counsel, to comfort, or to exhort, or to do any other thing requisite for our salvation, all those things we may learn plentifully from Scripture. There is abundantly enough, both for adults to eat, and children to suck. There is something appropriate for all ages, and for all ranks and all sorts of people.

These books therefore, ought to be much in our hands, in our eyes, in our ears, in our mouths, but most of all, in our hearts.

⊙ Apply

Do you come to the Bible just for stories and pithy words of comfort, or for the more serious tasks of learning, healing and salvation?

Do you think of reading the Bible as a chore, a massively useful exercise, or something else?

⊙ Pray

Thank God for revealing to us in the Bible our own situation before him, and the way of salvation.

Ask God to show you how comforting, healing and rebuking the Bible can be.

~ Notes and Prayers ~

Day

15

Spiritual Liberty

Galatians 5 v 1-6

with Martin Luther

I nstead of sin and death, Christ gives us righteousness and everlasting life, changing the bondage and terrors of the Law into liberty of conscience and gospel consolation.

Read Galatians 5 v 1-6

What do you think it means that Christ has set us free (v 1)?

What would the opposite of that freedom be?

Freedom from Fear

This passage speaks of that liberty by which Christ has made us free—not from an earthly bondage, or from the Babylonian captivity, or from the tyranny of the Turkish Muslim empire, but from God's everlasting wrath. For Christ has made us free, not civilly nor bodily, but divinely. That is to say, we are made free in such a way that our conscience is now free and quiet, not fearing the wrath of God to come.

Who is able to express what a thing it is when a man is assured in his heart that God neither is nor will be angry with him, but will be for ever a merciful and a loving Father to him for Christ's sake? This is indeed a marvellous and an incomprehensible liberty, to have the most high and sovereign Majesty so favourable to us that he does not only defend, maintain and support us in this life, but also, as touching our bodies, will so deliver us that our bodies, which are sown in corruption, in dishonour and infirmity, shall rise again in incorruption, in glory and power. This is an inestimable liberty, that we are made free from the wrath of God for ever.

Liberty from the Law

Let us learn therefore to magnify this our liberty purchased by Jesus Christ, the Son of God, by whom all things were created both in heaven and earth. This liberty he has purchased with no other price than with his own blood, to deliver us not from any bodily or earthly servitude, but from a spiritual and everlasting bondage under mighty and invincible tyrants—that is, the Law, sin, death and the devil—and so to reconcile us to God his Father.

Now, since these enemies are overcome, and we are reconciled to God by the death of his Son, it is certain that we are righteous before God, and that whatever we do, it pleases him. And although there are certain remnants of sin yet still in us, they are not laid to our charge, but pardoned for Christ's sake.

⊙ Apply

Are you clear in your own mind that simply by trusting in Christ alone you do not need to fear God's Judgment Day? If not, who could help you to think more about this?

Jesus has delivered us from servitude to the Law and sin, but do you feel the pull of those things in your heart still?

⊙ Pray

Praise the Lord Jesus that he has set us free from the slavery of sin and fear of judgment.

Ask God to help you not to voluntarily return to the slavery of the Law and of the devil.

~ Notes and Prayers ~

Freedom to Love

Galatians 5 v 7-15

with Martin Luther

S ome people carelessly turn the liberty of the Spirit into wanton sensuality, but they have lost Christ and Christian liberty and become slaves of the devil.

Read Galatians 5 v 7-15

What can you tell about the situation in the Galatian churches from this passage?

Why is spiritual freedom not just about "doing whatever I like" (v 13-15)?

Satan's Abuse of Grace

This evil is common and the most pernicious of all the evils that Satan stirs up in the doctrine of faith: namely, that in very many people he turns this liberty, by which Christ has made us free, into the liberty of the flesh. The apostle Jude also complains about this in his epistle: "For certain individuals," he says, "whose condemnation was written about long ago have secretly slipped in among you. They are ungodly people, who pervert the grace of our God into a licence for immorality" (Jude 4).

For the flesh is utterly ignorant of the doctrine of grace—that is to say, it does not know that we are made righteous not by works but by faith only, and that the Law has no authority over us. Therefore when it hears the doctrine of faith, it abuses it and turns it into sensuality, and by and by thus it reasons, "If we are without law, let us then live as we want, let us do no good, let us give nothing to the needy, and let us not suffer any evil for there is no law to constrain us or bind us to do so".

Liberty to Love, Not Lust

So there is danger on either side; albeit the one is more tolerable then the other. If grace or faith are not preached, no one can be saved—for it is faith alone which justifies and saves. On the other side, if faith is preached (as of necessity it must be), the majority of people understand the doctrine of faith carnally, and turn the liberty of the Spirit into the liberty of the flesh.

All boast themselves to be professors of the gospel, and all boast of Christian liberty; and yet serving their own lusts, they give themselves to covetousness, pleasures, pride, envy and such other vices. No one does their duty faithfully; no one charitably serves the needs of their brother. The grief of this makes me sometimes so impatient!

⊙ Apply

What would you say to someone who said justification by faith alone undermines any need for Christians to live moral lives?

In your own heart, do you sometimes excuse your own sins on the basis that you are saved by faith alone and not by works?

⊙ Pray

Confess to God any times when you may have turned the grace of the gospel into an opportunity for sin, or have been tempted to.

Ask God to help you love your neighbour as yourself, not as a way of being saved but as a way of using your freedom to please him.

~ Notes and Prayers ~

_____

_____

_____

_____

_____

_____

_____

_____

_____

_____

_____

_____

_____

_____

_____

_____

_____

_____

_____

_____

Day

I7

Spiritual
Battle

Galatians 5 v 16-26

with Martin Luther

N o Christian should be dismayed or discouraged when they feel in
themselves the battle of the flesh against the Spirit.

Read Galatians 5 v 16-26

What do you think it means to "live by the Spirit" (v 16)?

What is the opposite of that?

Flesh and Spirit

Let no one despair if they feel the flesh often stirring up a new battle against the
Spirit, or if they cannot quickly subdue the flesh and make it obedient to the Spirit.
I also wish myself to have a more valiant and constant heart, which might be able
boldly to scorn the threatenings of tyrants, the heresies and tumults which Satan
and his soldiers (the enemies of the gospel) stir up. But also that I might soon
shake off the vexations and anguish of spirit and might not fear the sharpness of
death, but receive and embrace it as a most friendly guest. Others also wrestle with
temptations and trials such as poverty, reproach, impatience, and such like.

When you feel this battle, resist in spirit and say, "I am a sinner, and I feel sin
in me, for I have not yet put off the flesh, in which sins dwells so long as it lives.
But I will obey the Spirit and not the flesh—that is, I will by faith and hope lay

hold on Christ, and by his word I will raise myself up, and will not fulfil the desire of the flesh."

Holy Desperation

I remember that Dr. Staupitius *(Luther's spiritual supervisor when he was a monk)* used to say, "I have vowed to God a thousand times that I would become a better man. But I never performed that which I vowed. From now on, I will make no such vow, for I have now learned by experience that I am not able to perform it. Unless, therefore, God is favourable and merciful to me for Christ's sake, I shall not be able with all my vows and all my good deeds, to stand before him."

This was not only a true, but also a godly and a holy desperation—and all those who want to be saved must confess this with heart and mouth. But let not those who feel the lust of the flesh despair of their salvation; because the more godly someone is, the more they will feel that battle.

⊙ Apply

When you next feel the battle between the flesh and the Spirit, will you give in or resist?

What would you say to someone who said they did not experience an internal battle such as Paul describes?

⊙ Pray

Pray for the Spirit's strength to enable you to keep waging war against the flesh.

Pray for the fruit of the Spirit (v 22-23) to be more and more evident in your life as you fight.

~ Notes and Prayers ~

Day 18

Greedy for Glory

Galatians 6 v 1-6

with Martin Luther

Paul rebukes the vanity of those who deceive themselves that they are "something", when really they are not.

Read Galatians 6 v 1-6

Why do the people described here need to be careful in how they think of themselves?

What might indicate that Paul is talking here especially to those who minister to others?

The Poison of Vainglory

Although it may be understood of the works of this life or civil conversation, yet principally the apostle speaks here of the work of ministry, and denounces those vainglorious heads who, with their fantastical opinions, do trouble well-instructed consciences.

Those who are infected with this poison of vainglory have no regard whether their work—that is to say, their ministry—is pure, simple and faithful or not. But this alone they seek, that they may have the praise of the people. So the false apostles, when they saw that Paul preached the gospel purely to the Galatians, and that they could not bring any better doctrine, they began to find fault with those things which he had faithfully taught them. By this subtlety they won the favour of the Galatians, and made them hate Paul.

Bewitching the People

The proud and vainglorious join these three vices together. First, they are greedy for glory. Secondly, they are marvellously witty and wily in finding fault with other people's doings and sayings, in order to purchase the love, the approval and the praise of the people. And thirdly, when they have made a name for themselves, they become so stout and full of stomach that they dare venture upon all things. Therefore they are pernicious and pestilent fellows, whom I hate even with my very heart—"for everyone looks out for their own interests, not those of Jesus Christ" (Philippians 2 v 21).

Against such people, Paul speaks here. Such vainglorious spirits teach the gospel so that they may win praise and estimation among people, that they may be counted excellent teachers. And when they have achieved this estimation, then they begin to rebuke the sayings and doings of others, and highly commend their own. By this subtlety they bewitch the minds of the people, who, because they have itching ears, are not only delighted with new opinions but also rejoice to see those teachers which they had before being abased and defaced by these new upstarts and glorious heads—and all because they loathe the word.

⊙ Apply

Do you think too highly of yourself and your spirituality, abilities or ministry?

Are you "marvellously witty and wily in finding fault with other people's doings and sayings"?

⊙ Pray

Confess to God if you have been too quick to criticise others to build your own reputation or if you are "greedy for glory".

Ask God to help you root out pride and vainglory from your own life.

~ Notes and Prayers ~

Day

19

Gospel Liberality

Galatians 6 v 6-10

with Martin Luther

Those who sow to please the Spirit will be blessed both in this life and the life to come, but those who wearily sow to the flesh will be accursed both now and in the future.

Read Galatians 6 v 6-10

What's in it for us if we do good works?

Why should we persist in them and not grow weary?

Funding Ministry

Here Paul preaches to the hearers of the word, commanding them to bestow all good things upon those who have taught and instructed them in the word. I have sometimes marvelled why the apostle commanded the churches so diligently to nourish their teachers. For within the Roman Catholic church I saw that everyone gave abundantly to the building and maintaining of lavish temples, and to the increase of the revenues of those who were appointed to their service.

Therefore I thought that Paul had commanded this in vain, seeing that all manner of good things were not only abundantly given to the clergy, but they also overflowed in wealth and riches. But now I know the cause why they had such abundance before, and why the pastors and ministers of the word are now in want.

For Satan can abide nothing less than the light of the gospel. Therefore when he sees that it begins to shine, he rages and goes about with all his might to quench it. And this he attempts two ways: first by lying spirits and force of tyrants; and then by poverty and famine. But because he could not oppress the gospel in this country (praised be God) by heretics and tyrants, he attempted to withdraw the livings of the ministers, so that they should forsake the ministry—and the miserable people being destitute of the word of God should become in time like savage, wild beasts.

Generosity to All

The apostle then passes from the particular to the general, and exhorts people generally to all good works. As if he should say, "Let us be liberal and bountiful, not only towards the ministers of the word, but also towards all others—and that without weariness". For it is an easy matter for someone to do good once or twice; but to continue and not be discouraged through the ingratitude of others, that is very hard. But in due time we shall reap. Wait and look for the harvest that is to come, and then no ingratitude will be able to pluck you away from well doing.

⊙ Apply

Are you generous in supporting the gospel ministry from which you benefit?

Have you grown weary in being generous to others, and do you need to remember the heavenly reward for good and faithful servants?

⊙ Pray

Pray for there to be sufficient finance to train and support more gospel ministers in your area.

Ask God to give you opportunities and strength to "do good to all people, especially to those who belong to the family of believers".

~ Notes and Prayers ~

Day
20

Crucified
to the World

Galatians 6 v 11-18

with Martin Luther

O ur glory is a different kind of glory from that which the world values. We rejoice in suffering, persecution and death; but they boast in power, riches and honour.

Read Galatians 6 v 11-18

What does Paul say his opponents in Galatia were most interested in (v 12-13)?

What was Paul most interested in (v 14-15)?

Damning the World

This is Paul's manner of speaking: "The world has been crucified to me"—that is, *I judge the world to be damned.* "And I [am crucified] to the world"—that is, *The world judges me to be damned.* Thus we crucify and condemn one another. I abhor all the doctrine, righteousness, and works of the world as the poison of the devil. The world detests my doctrine and deeds, and judges me to be a seditious, a pernicious, a pestilential fellow, and a heretic.

So, at this day, the world is crucified to us, and we to the world. We curse and condemn all human traditions concerning masses, holy orders, vows, works, and all the abominations of heretics, as the dirt of the devil. They in return persecute and kill us as destroyers of religion and troublers of the public peace.

The monks dreamed that the world was crucified to them when they entered into their monasteries. But by this means Christ is crucified and not the world. Indeed, the world is delivered from being crucified, and is the more quickened, by that opinion of holiness and trust which religious people had in their own righteousness. Most foolishly and wickedly therefore was this sentence of the apostle twisted to be about entering into monasteries.

Judging Rightly

Paul speaks here of a high matter, of great importance. That is to say, what every faithful person judges to be the wisdom, righteousness and power of God, the world condemns as the greatest folly, wickedness and weakness. And on the other side, that which the world judges to be the highest religion and service of God, the faithful know to be nothing else but lamentable and horrible blasphemy against God.

Now, in the Scriptures, "the world" not only signifies ungodly and wicked people, but the very best, the wisest and holiest that are of the world. But the godly condemn the world, and the world condemns the godly. Yet the godly have the right judgment on their side.

⊙ Apply

Do you value what the world around you values, and care about what it cares about?

Do you care about "impressing people by means of the flesh" more than you should?

⊙ Pray

Ask the Spirit to show you how you are adopting the values of the world instead of judging everything in the light of the cross.

Thank God for everything we have learned from Galatians, and from Martin Luther!

~ Notes and Prayers ~

Day
21

Building on the Rock

Matthew 7 v 24-27

with Thomas Cranmer

The affection we have for the transitory things of this world will only be trumped by a greater desire for heavenly things if we diligently read God's word.

Read Matthew 7 v 24-27

What is assumed in both parts of Jesus' parable?

What is the real difference between a wise and a foolish man?

A More Excellent Treasure

The Scripture of God is the heavenly meat of our souls. The hearing and keeping of it makes us blessed, sanctifies us, and makes us holy; it converts our souls; it is a light to our feet; it is a sure, a constant, and a perpetual instrument of salvation; it gives wisdom to the humble and lowly hearts; it comforts, makes glad, cheers and cherishes our consciences; it is a more excellent jewel or treasure than any gold or precious stone; it is sweeter than honey, or honeycomb; it is called the best part, which Mary chose (Luke 10 v 42), for it has in it everlasting comfort.

The words of holy Scripture are called words of everlasting life, for they are God's instrument, ordained for that purpose. They have power to convert through God's promise, and they are effective, through God's assistance. Being received in a faithful heart, they have ever a heavenly spiritual-working in them—they are lively and mighty in operation, and sharper than any two-edged sword, dividing asunder the soul and the spirit, the joints and the marrow (Hebrews 4 v 12).

A Wise Builder

Christ calls him a wise builder that builds on his word, on his sure and substantial foundation. By this word of God we shall be judged: for the word that I speak (says Christ) is what shall judge in the last day. The person who keeps the word of Christ is promised the love and favour of God, and that they shall be the dwelling place or temple of the blessed Trinity.

Whoever is diligent to read this word, and in their heart to print what they read— the great affection for the transitory things of this world shall be diminished in them, and the great desire of heavenly things (that are therein promised of God) shall increase.

⊙ Apply

Since there will be troubles and difficulties in all our lives, are you committed to regular, careful reading of God's word, which is so vital for spiritual stability?

Have you "printed" what you've learned this week from the Bible on your heart? How can you make sure you don't just forget what you've heard?

⊙ Pray

Ask God to help you build your life on his word, so your faith will withstand the assaults of the world, the flesh and the devil.

Ask him to help two or three of your friends to do the same, and to increase their desire for heavenly things.

~ Notes and Prayers ~

Day
22

In the Beginning

Genesis I v I-I9

with John Calvin

For the next three weeks, we will be reading through parts of Genesis (traditionally said to be written by Moses) with the expert help of John Calvin's commentary.

Read Genesis I v I-I9

What do you admire most about the design of God's creation?

What is the difference between Genesis 1 and a modern scientific textbook?

Admiring God's Works

"God saw that the light was good" (v 4). Here God is introduced by Moses as surveying his work, that he might take pleasure in it. But he does it for our sake, to teach us that God has made nothing without a certain reason and design. And we ought not so to understand the words of Moses as if God did not know that his work was good until it was finished. But the meaning of the passage is that the work, such as we now see it, was approved by God. Therefore nothing remains for us, but to agree with this judgment of God. And this admonition is very useful. For we ought to apply all our senses to the admiring contemplation of the works of God.

The Miracle of Clouds

"Let there be a vault/expanse" (v 6). We see clouds suspended in the air, which threaten to fall upon our heads, yet leave us space to breathe. Those who deny that this is effected by the wonderful providence of God are vainly inflated with the folly of their own minds. We know indeed that the rain is naturally produced; but the deluge sufficiently shows how speedily we might be overwhelmed by the bursting of the clouds, if the cataracts of heaven were not closed by the hand of God.

Astronomy Is Good

"God made two great lights" (v 16). Moses wrote in a popular style things which, without instruction, all ordinary persons endued with common sense are able to understand. But astronomers investigate with great labour whatever the intelligence of the human mind can comprehend. Nevertheless, this study is not to be rejected, nor this science to be condemned because some frantic persons boldly reject whatever is unknown to them. For astronomy is not only pleasant, but also very useful to be known. It cannot be denied that this art unfolds the admirable wisdom of God. Wherefore, as ingenious people who have expended useful labour on this subject are to be honoured, so they who have leisure and capacity ought not to neglect this kind of exercise.

⊙ Apply

Next time you go outside, ponder how amazing it is that the clouds don't suddenly burst and fall upon you!

What other miracles of providence in the design of creation do you admire?

⊙ Pray

Thank God for the natural sciences that we use to investigate his admirable wisdom and design in creation.

Ask God to help you understand and appreciate those aspects of creation that you may previously have taken for granted.

~ Notes and Prayers ~

Day
23

God Blesses Mankind

Genesis 1 v 20-31

with John Calvin

G od made mankind and blessed them. In the symmetry of God's works there is the highest perfection, to which nothing can be added.

Read Genesis 1 v 20-31

What is the place of humanity in God's creation?

What does God provide for them?

God Takes Counsel with Himself

"Let us make mankind" (v 26). With these words, God "takes counsel" and discusses the creation of mankind in his image. By doing so, he commends to our attention the dignity of our nature, and testifies that he is about to undertake something great and wonderful. But since the Lord needs no other counsellor, there can be no doubt that he consulted with himself. Christians, therefore, properly contend, from this testimony, that there exists a plurality of Persons in the Godhead. God summons no foreign counsellor.

The Image of God

"In our image" (v 26). It is too crude to say that our resemblance to God is to be found simply in the shape or form of the human body, as some people think.

Others proceed with a little more subtlety, and maintain that the image of God is in the human body because in it God's admirable workmanship shines brightly. But this opinion is by no means in accordance with Scripture. Others see God's image in the dominion which was given to mankind in order that they might, in a certain sense, act as God's representative in the government of the world; but they are not correct either. This is only a very small part of what it means to be made in the image of God.

Since the image of God was destroyed in us by the Fall, we may judge from its restoration what it originally had been. Paul says that we are transformed into the image of God *by the gospel*. And, according to him, spiritual regeneration is nothing else than the restoration of God's image in us (see Colossians 3 v 10; Ephesians 4 v 23-24).

God's Blessing

"God blessed them" (v 28). God certainly did not intend that mankind should be slenderly and sparingly sustained; but rather, by these words, he promises a liberal abundance, which should leave nothing lacking for a sweet and pleasant life. For Moses relates how generous the Lord had been to them, in bestowing on them all things which they could desire, that their ingratitude might have the less excuse. After the workmanship of the world had received the last finishing touch, God pronounces it perfectly good.

⊙ Apply

Do you agree that there are hints of more than one "Person" in the Godhead, in Genesis 1?

Ponder the fact that God has given us "a liberal abundance" of good things in creation, for a sweet and pleasant life.

⊙ Pray

Thank God for his goodness in creating humanity, male and female, in his own image.

Praise God for the wonderful blessings he has given us, even in this fallen world.

~ Notes and Prayers ~

Man and Wife

Genesis 2 v 18-25

with John Calvin

There are many difficulties in our relationships, which are the fruits of our fallen nature, but some residue of God's original good design remains.

Read Genesis 2 v 18-25

Why did God make Eve (v 18, 20)?

Do you think this was just a one-off, or the start of an ongoing pattern?

Alone

"It is not good for the man to be alone" (v 18). Moses now explains the design of God in creating woman—namely, that there should be human beings on the earth who might cultivate mutual society between themselves. Man was formed to be a social animal. The human race could not exist without the woman.

Although God pronounced, concerning Adam, that it would not be profitable for him to be alone, yet I do not restrict this declaration to him alone, but rather regard it as a common law of our vocation. So everyone ought to receive it as said to them, that solitude is not good, though there are some who are able by God's grace to remain single (see 1 Corinthians 7).

Together

"I will make a helper suitable for him" (v 18). There is a vulgar proverb which says woman is a necessary evil. But the voice of God is rather to be heard, which declares that woman is given as a companion and an associate to the man, to assist him to live well.   .

In the current corrupt state of mankind, this blessing of God is neither perceived nor flourishes. But if the integrity of man had remained to this day such as it was from the beginning, that divine institution would be clearly discerned, and the sweetest harmony would reign in marriage. The husband would look up with reverence to God, the woman would be a faithful assistant to him in this, and both with one consent would cultivate a holy, a friendly, and a peaceful relationship.

Now, it has happened by our fault and by the corruption of nature that this happiness of marriage has in a great measure perished or, at least, is mixed and infected with many inconveniences. Hence arise strifes, troubles, sorrows, disagreement and discord, and a boundless sea of evils. Still, marriage was not capable of being so far spoiled by our depravity that the blessing which God has once sanctioned by his word should be utterly abolished and extinguished. Therefore, some residue of divine good remains, like when a fire is apparently smothered, but some sparks still glitter.

⊙ Apply

What do you think it means for us to be "social animals"?

Calvin rejects a vulgar proverb and says we should listen to God's word instead. What other worldly sayings or attitudes about male-female relationships need correcting?

⊙ Pray

Thank God for all the relationships you have in life which mean you are not entirely alone (especially for your wife or husband, if you have one).

Ask God to help you cultivate holy, friendly, and peaceful relationships that will help others "look up with reverence to God".

~ Notes and Prayers ~

_____

_____

_____

_____

_____

_____

_____

_____

_____

_____

_____

_____

_____

_____

_____

_____

_____

_____

_____

_____

_____

_____

Day
25

The Fall

Genesis 3 v 1-7

with John Calvin

P ride was the beginning of all evils, and by proudly rejecting God's word in monstrous ingratitude, the human race was enslaved to the devil.

Read Genesis 3 v 1-7

In what ways do you think sin is a rejection of God's ordering for creation?

What do you think was the essence of Adam and Eve's sin?

The World Turned Upside Down

In this chapter, Moses explains that man, after he had been deceived by Satan, revolted from his Maker. He became entirely changed and so degenerate that the image of God, in which he had been formed, was obliterated. Moses then declares that the whole world fell together with him and that much of its original excellence was destroyed.

The baseness of human ingratitude is more clearly perceived in this: that although Adam and Eve knew that all animals were given by the hand of God into subjection to them (Genesis 1 v 26), they allowed themselves to be led away by one of their own slaves into rebellion against God. As often as they saw any one of the animals which were in the world, they ought to have been reminded of the supreme authority and singular goodness of God. But, on the contrary, when they saw the serpent in rebellion against his Creator, not only did they neglect to punish it but in violation of all lawful order they subjected and devoted themselves to it. They became

83

participators in the same rebellion. What can be imagined more dishonourable than this extreme depravity?

The design of Moses, therefore, was to show in a few words how greatly our present condition differs from our original state in creation. He wished us to learn, with humble confession of our fault, to lament our evils.

Forsaking God's Word

What was the sin of Adam and Eve? They revolted from God, when, having forsaken his word, they lent their ears to the falsehoods of Satan. From this we infer that God will be seen and adored in his word and, therefore, that all reverence for him is shaken off when his word is despised. The word of God obtains its due honour only with a few, but some rush onward with impunity in contempt of this word, and still assign to themselves a chief rank among the worshippers of God. But God does not manifest himself to us otherwise than through the word. So, unbelief was the root of defection; just as faith alone unites us to God.

⊙ Apply

Are you tempted to reject or marginalise God's word in favour of some other voices in your decision-making processes?

By subjecting themselves to an animal, Adam and Eve overturned the order God had made for them in the garden. In what ways does your personal sin subvert the way things were designed by God in his goodness to be?

⊙ Pray

Ask God to help you understand more of the depths of sin and what it has done to the world.

Confess to God your own disbelief and rejection of his word.

~ Notes and Prayers ~

Sin
Exposed

Genesis 3 v 8-24

with John Calvin

A dam and Eve aggravate their crime with frivolous and ungodly defences and so, along with the serpent, they are judged by God.

Read Genesis 3 v 8-24

How do Adam and Eve try to hide and excuse their sin?

Why does God bar the way back to the tree of life (v 24)?

Flimsy Leaves

Verse 8. As soon as the voice of God sounds, Adam and Eve perceive that the leaves by which they thought themselves well protected are of no avail. The difference between good and evil is engraved on the hearts of all, as Paul teaches (Romans 2 v 15). But all bury the disgrace of their vices under flimsy leaves until God, by his voice, inwardly strikes their consciences. Hence, after God had shaken them out of their dullness, their alarmed consciences compelled them to hear his voice.

Dreadful Alienation

Verse 17. The Lord determined that his anger should, like a deluge, overflow all parts of the earth. So wherever man might look, the atrocity of his sin should meet his eyes. Before the fall, the state of the world was a most fair and delightful mirror of the divine favour and paternal indulgence towards mankind. Now, in all the elements we perceive that we are cursed. And although (as David says) the earth is still full of the mercy of God (Psalm 33 v 5), yet, at the same time, there appear manifest signs of his dreadful alienation from us. If we are unmoved by these, then we betray our blindness and indifference. Only, so that sadness and horror should not overwhelm us, the Lord sprinkles everywhere the tokens of his goodness.

Excommunicated

Verses 22-24. By depriving Adam and Eve of the symbol (the tree of life), God also takes away the thing signified by it. A solemn excommunication is pronounced so that they would understand themselves to be deprived of their former life. It was not that the Lord would cut them off from all hope of salvation, but he did not want them to entertain a vain hope of the perpetuity of the life they had lost. They could not actually enjoy life against the will of God, even if they devoured the whole tree of life. There never was any intrinsic effectiveness in the tree. But by taking it away, he wanted them to seek new assistance elsewhere. They could only recover life by the death of Christ.

⊘ Apply

Do you blame others for your own sin, as Adam and Eve tried to transfer blame?

What signs of the curse, and signs of God's mercy, do you see in the world today?

⊘ Pray

Thank God that in his righteous anger against sin he remains gracious and merciful.

Ask God to give you an understanding of sin and judgment that leads to greater humility and repentance.

~ Notes and Prayers ~

Day

27

Cain
and Abel

Genesis 4 v 1-16

with John Calvin

S ince the whole human race is rejected by God after the Fall, there is no
other way of reconciliation to divine favour than through God-given faith.

Read Genesis 4 v 1-16

Why do you think God accepted Abel's offering (v 4)?

Why do you think God did not accept Cain's offering (v 5)?

Abel and His Offering

Verse 4. The writer of Hebrews says Abel's sacrifice was accepted by faith (Hebrews
11 v 4). Filled with the good odour of faith, it had a sweet-smelling aroma to God.
Moses does not simply state that the *worship* which Abel had paid was pleasing to
God, but he begins with the *person* of the offerer (v 4). By this he signifies that God
will regard no works with favour unless the one who does them has already been
accepted and approved by him. And no wonder; for "people look at the outward
appearance, but the LORD looks at the heart" (1 Samuel 16 v 7). Therefore, he only
assesses works as they proceed from the fountain of the heart.

This is why he not only rejects but abhors the sacrifices of the wicked, however
splendid they may appear in the eyes of men. All works done before faith, whatever
splendour of righteousness may appear in them, are nothing but mere sins, being

89

defiled from their roots. They are offensive to the Lord, whom nothing can please without inward purity of heart. For this must be received as a settled point—in the judgment of God, no respect is had to works until someone is received into his favour. Moreover, since faith is a gracious gift of God, and a special illumination of the Spirit, then it is easy to infer that his mere grace goes before us, just as if he had raised us from the dead.

Cain and His Offering

Verse 5. Cain conducted himself as hypocrites are accustomed to do. He wished to appease God, as one discharging a debt, by external sacrifices, without the least intention of dedicating himself to God. But this is true worship, to offer ourselves as spiritual sacrifices to God. When God sees such hypocrisy, combined with gross and manifest mockery of himself, it is not surprising that he hates it, and is unable to bear it. For it is his will, first to have us devoted to himself; he then seeks our works in testimony of our obedience to him, but only in the second place.

⊙ Apply

Have you ever tried to "appease God, as one discharging a debt" without being truly devoted to God?

Romans 8 v 8 says that "those who are in the realm of the flesh cannot please God". How do you feel about this idea?

⊙ Pray

Ask God to help you love and trust him sincerely from the heart.

Ask God to help you show your heartfelt love for him in appropriately obedient ways.

~ Notes and Prayers ~

Sweeter
Than Honey

Psalm 119 v 97-104

with Thomas Cranmer

Whoever gives their mind to the holy Scriptures, with diligent study and fervent desire, will not be destitute of help.

Read Psalm 119 v 97-104

Meditating on God's word makes the psalm-writer wiser than various people. Who?

What is the result of understanding God's word?

Understanding Mysteries

If we lack a learned person to instruct and teach us, yet God himself from above will give light to our minds, and teach us those things which are necessary for us, and of which we are ignorant.

Many things in Scripture are spoken in obscure mysteries. Yet there is nothing spoken under dark mysteries in one place, but the self same thing in other places is spoken more familiarly and plainly, to the capacity both of learned and unlearned. And those things in Scripture that are plain to understand, and necessary for salvation, everyone's duty is to learn them, to print them in memory, and effectually to exercise them. And as for the obscure mysteries, it is our duty to be contented to be ignorant in them, until such time as it shall please God, to open those things to us.

Making the Most of Our Privileges

In the meantime, if anyone lacks either aptitude or opportunity, God will not at-tribute it to their folly. Yet it is not fitting that such as are able to read should set aside reading simply because some others are not able to read. By Scripture, all are changed: the weak are strengthened, and the strong are comforted. So that surely, none are enemies to the reading of God's word except those who are either so ig-norant that they do not know how wholesome a thing it is, or else are so sick that they hate the most comfortable medicine that would heal them, or so ungodly that they would wish the people still to continue in blindness and ignorance of God.

God's holy word is one of God's chief and principal benefits, given and declared to mankind here on earth. So let us with fear and reverence lay up (in the chest of our hearts) these necessary and fruitful lessons. Let us night and day muse, meditate, and contemplate them. Let us ruminate, and (as it were) chew the cud, that we may have the sweet juice, spiritual effect, honey, kernel, taste, comfort, and consolation of them.

⊙ Apply

What should we do when we come across parts of the Bible that we find difficult to understand?

How could you be more diligent and fervent in your study of God's precious word?

⊙ Pray

Thank God for the great and special gift of his word, which brings light and comfort to us.

Ask God to help you unravel and enjoy the parts of the Bible which you have found most difficult to understand or obey recently.

~ Notes and Prayers ~

_____

_____

_____

_____

_____

_____

_____

_____

_____

_____

_____

_____

_____

_____

_____

_____

_____

_____

_____

_____

_____

_____

The Flood

Genesis 6 v 5-8

with John Calvin

G od was neither too harsh nor too hasty in exacting punishment from the
wicked people of the world.

Read Genesis 6 v 5-8

Why do you think the description of human sin is so lavish?

What does it mean here for God to grieve and be sorry that he made us (v 6-7)?

The Lord Saw

God was not induced to destroy the world merely for a slight cause. "The LORD saw",
(v 5) indicates long-continued patience. God did not proclaim his sentence to destroy humanity until he had well observed and long considered their case, and saw
them to be past recovery. A vast wickedness reigned everywhere, so that the whole
earth was covered with it. And so we perceive that it was not overwhelmed with a
deluge of waters until it had first been immersed in the pollution of wickedness.

Continual Depravity

Wickedness was too deeply seated in people's hearts to leave any hope of repentance. Moses teaches us that the mind of humanity was thoroughly saturated with
sin. The world had then become so hardened in its wickedness, and was so far
from any amendment or from entertaining any feeling of penitence, that it grew

worse and worse as time advanced. This was not the folly of a few days, but the habitual depravity which the children transmitted from their parents to their descendants. This is not a mere complaint concerning a few men, but a description of the human mind when left to itself, destitute of the Spirit of God.

God's Heart

Moses introduces God as speaking in a human way, by a figure of speech which ascribes human affections to God. Certainly God is not sorrowful or sad, but remains forever in his celestial and happy repose. Yet because it could not otherwise be known how great is God's hatred and detestation of sin, therefore the Spirit accommodates himself to our capacity. There is no need for us to involve ourselves in thorny and difficult questions. It is obvious that these words of repentance and grief are used to teach us that God was so offended by the atrocious wickedness of mankind, *as if* they had wounded his heart with mortal grief. In order more effectually to pierce our hearts, he clothes himself with our affections. So unless we wish to provoke God, and to put him to grief, let us learn to abhor and to flee from sin.

⊘ Apply

Are your feelings about sin in your heart and in the world the same as those God is represented as having here?

Do you really think that human sin is as bad as Moses makes it out to be?

⊙ Pray

Confess to God the evil intentions and thoughts of your own heart.

Thank God that he has saved you by grace alone, despite your sin.

~ Notes and Prayers ~

The Tower of Babel

Genesis 11 v 1-9

with John Calvin

As soon as mortals are inflated above measure, they wage war with God. But the division of languages is inflicted as a punishment for their conspiracy.

Read Genesis 11 v 1-9

What was it that drove them to build the tower (v 4)?

Why do you think God chose to punish them in this particular way?

Proud Contempt

Some people speculate that the tower of Babel was built as a refuge and protection in case God should determine to overwhelm the earth with a deluge again. But they have no other guide, that I can see, but the dream of their own brain. For Moses says no such thing. Rather, he speaks of their mad ambitions and proud contempt of God. They wish to have an immortal name on earth; and thus they build, as if in opposition to the will of God. Ambition not only does injury to mankind, but exalts itself even against God, waging war against him. To build a tower was not in itself so great a crime; but to raise an eternal monument to themselves, which might endure throughout all ages, was a proof of headstrong pride, joined with contempt of God.

Earthly Ambition

Moses intimates that they had not been induced to commence this work on account of the ease with which it could be accomplished nor on account of any other advantages. Rather, they contended with great and arduous difficulties, by which means their guilt became more aggravated. They wear themselves out in vain on a difficult and laborious enterprise, and like madmen they rush impetuously against God. Difficulty often deters us from necessary works; but these people, when they had neither stones nor mortar, do not hesitate to attempt the raising of an edifice which may transcend the clouds. We are taught therefore to what length people's lust will hurry them, when they indulge their ambition. This is the perpetual infatuation of the world: to neglect heaven, and to seek immortality on earth, where everything is fading and temporary.

Disgrace

God declares that he is at perpetual war with the unmeasured audacity of men; anything we undertake without his approval will end miserably. People had already been spread abroad, and this ought not to be regarded as a punishment. But now the principal bond of conjunction between them was cut. Behold what they gained by their foolish ambition to acquire a name! He brands them with eternal disgrace.

⊙ Apply

What is it that drives your own ambitions?

Are your ambitions merely earthly, "where everything is fading and temporary"?

⊙ Pray

Confess to God where your ambitions in life have been driven by personal pride.

Ask God to give you godly ambitions which serve his kingdom and glory more than your own.

~ Notes and Prayers ~

Day
31

The Call
of Abram

Genesis 12 v 1-3

with John Calvin

G od calls Abram (later to be called Abraham), who was worshipping other gods, to leave his former life and be blessed by giving up everything to follow the true God.

Read Genesis 12 v 1-3

Why do you think God chooses to bless Abram?

Why does this blessing come with a command to leave everything else behind?

Gracious Call

Abram's calling is an instance of the gracious mercy of God. We must always recall (see Joshua 24 v 2) that Abram was plunged in the filth of idolatry. And now God freely stretches forth his hand to bring back the wanderer. He deigns to open his sacred mouth that he may show to one deceived by Satan's schemes the way of salvation.

It is wonderful that a man, miserable and lost, should have the covenant of life placed in his possession, and he himself constituted the father of all the faithful. But this is done with a deliberate design, in order that the grace of God might be more conspicuously revealed. For Abram is an example of the calling of us all, that by the mere mercy of God things which are "nothing" are raised up to be "something".

The Test of Faith

The sweetness of their native soil holds nearly all people bound to itself, so God strenuously persists in his command to "leave your country". He does this to thoroughly penetrate the mind of Abram, who is still more deeply affected when he hears that he must renounce his kindred and his father's house. Yet it is not to be supposed that God takes a cruel pleasure in the trouble of his servants; but he thus tries all their affections, that he may not leave any lurking-places undiscovered in their hearts.

We see many persons zealous for a short time, who afterwards become frozen. Why is this, but because they build without a foundation? Therefore God determined thoroughly to rouse all Abram's senses, that he might undertake nothing rashly, lest, changing his mind soon afterwards, he should veer with the wind and return.

Therefore, if we desire to follow God with constancy, it is good for us carefully to meditate on all the inconveniences, difficulties and dangers which await us. A hasty zeal may produce fading flowers, but from a deep and well-fixed root of piety we may bring forth fruit in our whole life.

⊙ Apply

Do you sometimes think that God chose you because of something great or good about you?

What has God asked you to leave behind or abandon to follow him?

⊙ Pray

Praise God that he chose us to follow him despite the fact that we were "nothing", or even that we were against him.

Ask God to help you follow him wholeheartedly, whatever you may have to leave behind.

~ Notes and Prayers ~

Abram's Shield and Reward

Genesis 15

with John Calvin

The one who has God himself for their inheritance does not exult in fading joy, but enjoys the solid happiness of eternal life by embracing God as their Father.

Read Genesis 15

What does God promise to Abram in this passage?

What does verse 6 mean by "credited it to him as righteousness"?

Our Reward

In calling himself Abram's "reward" (v 1), God teaches Abram to be satisfied with himself alone. By this voice, God daily speaks to all his faithful ones. Having once undertaken to defend us, he will take care to preserve us in safety under his hand and to protect us by his power. God also ascribes to himself the office of a shield, to make himself the protector of our salvation. So we should not be excessively fearful in any dangers.

Since people surrounded with innumerable desires of the flesh are at times unstable, and too much addicted to the love of the present life, God declares that he alone is sufficient for the perfection of a happy life to the faithful. It ought to be deeply engraved on our minds that in God alone we have the highest and complete perfection of all good things.

We shall be truly happy when God is propitious to us. For he not only pours upon us the abundance of his kindness, but offers himself to us, that we may enjoy him. Now what is there more which people can desire when they really enjoy God?

Whoever is fully persuaded that their life is protected by the hand of God, and that they can never be miserable while God is gracious to them, will find the best remedy for all evils. Not that the faithful can be entirely free from fear and care, as long as they are tossed by the tempests of this life; but because the storm is hushed in their own breast, faith triumphs over fear.

Credited to Him as Righteousness

The faith of Abram is commended, because by it he embraced the promise of God. It is also commended because by it Abram obtained righteousness in the sight of God, and that by imputation. Just as we understand that they to whom sin is imputed are guilty before God, so those to whom he imputes righteousness are approved by him as just. So Abram was received into the number and rank of the just by the imputation of righteousness.

⊙ Apply

What do you think you need to be truly happy?

Do you think of knowing God himself as the greatest blessing you have, or are you more fixated on the other things he gives you?

⊙ Pray

Praise God that he has given us himself, as our shield and reward.

Ask God to help you look to him more and more for your happiness, rather than to your secret sins and desires.

~ Notes and Prayers ~

Day
33

Escape from Sodom

Genesis 19 v 12-26

with John Calvin

The faithful ought to endeavour with greater earnestness to prepare themselves to follow God and beware lest with deaf ears they disregard his warnings.

Read Genesis 19 v 12-26

Lot was the nephew of Abram, now called Abraham. Why do you think Lot was so slow in leaving the city he knew was about to be destroyed?

Why was Lot's wife turned into a pillar of salt?

Read 2 Peter 2 v 7. How does the Bible view Lot, flawed though he was?

Lot's Sloth

Having praised the faith and piety of Lot, Moses shows that something human still adhered to him; because the angels hastened him, when he was lingering. A multiplicity of cares and fears disturb his anxious mind. He does not consider that he must act like persons shipwrecked, who, in order that they may come safe into port, cast their cargo into the sea. He does not doubt that God is speaking the truth, nor does he refuse to go; but entangled with many cares, he who ought to have run hastily and without delay, moves with slow and halting pace.

Here the Spirit of God presents to us, as in a mirror, our own tardiness—in order that we, shaking off all sloth, may prepare ourselves for prompt obedience, as soon as the heavenly voice sounds in our ears.

The Lord's Hand

It is often necessary for us to be forcibly drawn away from scenes which we do not willingly leave. Riches, honours, or other things of that kind may prove an obstacle to many. So if they are robbed of their fortune, or reduced to a lower rank, let them realise that the Lord has laid hold of their hand because words and exhortations had not sufficiently profited them. The mercy of God struggled with the sluggishness of Lot. Left to himself, he would, by lingering, have brought down upon his own head the destruction which was already near.

Lot's Wife

Lot's wife was moved by some evil desire; she did not cheerfully leave Sodom to hasten to the place where God called her. Christ commands us to remember Lot's wife (Luke 17 v 32), lest the allurements of the world should draw us aside from meditation on the heavenly life. It is therefore probable that she, being discontented with the favour God had granted her, glided into unholy desires, of which thing also her tardiness was a sign.

They sin no less grievously, who, being delivered not from Sodom but from hell, fix their eyes on some other object than the prize of their high calling.

⊙ Apply

What cares and fears prevent you from moving more earnestly in the direction you know God wants you to go?

What allurements of this world are distracting you and making you discontent with God?

⊙ Pray

Confess to God your sluggish obedience to his word.

Ask God to help you keep your mind focused on the city to come, whose "architect and builder" is God himself.

~ Notes and Prayers ~

_____

_____

_____

_____

_____

_____

_____

_____

_____

_____

_____

_____

_____

_____

_____

_____

_____

_____

_____

The Binding of Isaac

Genesis 22 v 1-19

with John Calvin

G od tests the faith which Abraham has placed in his word, by a counter-assault of the word itself, which seemed to threaten the whole salvation of the world.

Read Genesis 22 v 1-19

Beyond the sheer horror of Abraham killing his own son, why would the death of Isaac be such a huge problem for Abraham and his story?

How do you think Abraham resolved any conflicts in his mind here?

Abraham's Faith

Not only is the death of his son announced to him, but Abraham is commanded with his own hand to slay him. It is as if he were required not only to throw aside but to cut in pieces or cast into the fire the charter of his salvation, and to have nothing left for himself but death and hell. But it may be asked how, under the guidance of faith, he could be brought to sacrifice his son, seeing that what was proposed to him was in opposition to that word of God on which it is necessary for faith to rely (Genesis 17 v 19; 21 v 12)?

To this question the writer of Hebrews answers, that Abraham's confidence in the word of God remained unshaken. He hoped that God would be able to cause the promised blessing to spring up, even out of the dead ashes of his son (Hebrews 11 v 17-19). His mind, however, must of necessity have been severely crushed and violently agitated when the *command* and the *promise* of God were conflicting within him.

Although he did not immediately discover how the contradiction might be removed he, nevertheless, by hope, reconciled the command with the promise. Being persuaded that God was faithful, he left the unknown issue to divine providence.

Abraham's Example

It remains for every one of us to apply this example to ourselves. The Lord, indeed, is so indulgent to our weakness that he does not thus severely and sharply try our faith. Yet he intended, in the father of all the faithful, to propose an example by which he might call us to a general trial of faith. For faith, which is more precious than gold and silver, ought not to lie idle without trial (1 Peter 1 v 7).

Experience teaches that each will be tried by God, according to the measure of their faith. At the same time also we may observe that God tests his servants, not only when he subdues the affections of the flesh, but when he reduces all their senses to nothing, that he may lead them to a complete renunciation of themselves.

⊙ Apply

Would you trust and obey, if God's word commanded you to do something but you didn't understand how it would work out?

What do you think is the most difficult test of faith which God might ask of you?

⊙ Pray

Praise God that he provided a ram in place of Isaac, and the sacrifice of his own Son, Jesus, on the cross in our place.

Ask God to give you strength to trust and obey him, whatever comes your way.

~ Notes and Prayers ~

Day

35

The Misery of Humanity

Romans 3 v 9-20

with John Harpsfield

G od knows best what we are and what we ought to be called. "There is no one righteous, not even one."

Read Romans 3 v 9-20

Are some people better than others in God's eyes?

How can we find out how sinful we are?

We Are Dust

The Holy Spirit, in writing the holy Scripture, is in nothing more diligent than to pull down man's vainglory and pride which, of all vices, is most universally grafted in all mankind. And therefore we read in many places of Scripture many notable lessons against this old rooted vice, to teach us the most commendable virtue of humility, how to know ourselves, and to remember what we are of ourselves.

In the book of Genesis, Almighty God gives us all a title and name in our great grand-father Adam, which ought to admonish us all to consider what we are, and where we came from. He says, "By the sweat of your brow you will eat your food until you return to the ground, since from it you were taken; for dust you are and to dust you will return" (Genesis 3 v 19). Here (as in a mirror) we may learn to know ourselves to be but ground, earth and ashes—and that to earth and ashes we shall return.

It is not without great cause that the Scripture of God so many times calls all of us here in this world by this word: "earth". "O earth, earth, earth" says Jeremiah, "hear the word of the LORD" (Jeremiah 22 v 29, KJV). This our right name, vocation, and title—"earth, earth, earth"—pronounced by the prophet, shows what we are indeed, regardless of whatever style, title or dignity people might use to describe us. Thus he who knows best plainly named us, both what we are and what we ought of right to be called.

Sinners by Nature

The Scripture shuts up all under sin, that the promise by the faith of Jesus Christ should be given to those who believe. The Apostle Paul in many places paints us in our true colours, calling us the "children of [the] wrath [of God]" when we are born (Ephesians 2 v 3, ESV), saying also that we cannot think a good thought of ourselves, much less speak well or do well of ourselves. And the wise man says in the book of Proverbs, "The righteous fall seven times" (Proverbs 24 v 16).

⊙ Apply

What would you say to someone who claimed that people are basically good on the inside?

Ponder what would happen to the world if God left us entirely to our own devices and desires.

⊙ Pray

Ask God for the "most commendable virtue of humility": to know yourself truly.

Pray for his forgiveness for ways in which you have erred and strayed like a lost sheep.

~ Notes and Prayers ~

Isaac
Blesses Jacob

Genesis 27 v 1-29

with John Calvin

G od allowed Isaac to be deceived, in order to show that it was not by the will
of man that Jacob was raised up.

Read Genesis 27 v 1-29

Why do you think Moses spends so long telling this almost childish story of deception?

Did God bless Jacob because he was so clever and deceitful?

Cheating

In this chapter Moses recounts a history which does not appear to be of great utility. It amounts to this: Esau having gone out at his father's command to hunt, Jacob in his brother's clothing was, through the cunning of his mother, induced to obtain by stealth the blessing due by right to the firstborn. It seems even like child's play to present to his father a goat instead of venison, to pass himself off as hairy by putting on skins and pretending to be his brother, to get the blessing by a lie.

But Moses does not in vain pause over this narrative as a most serious matter. We must observe that when Jacob received the blessing from his father, this token confirmed to him the oracle by which the Lord had preferred him to his brother (Genesis 25 v 23). For the blessing here spoken of was not a mere prayer—rather, it made manifest the grace of election.

Election

The preference which God gave to Jacob over his brother Esau was not granted as a reward for his merits, neither was it obtained by his own industry. It proceeded from the mere grace of God himself. The disparity of condition certainly cannot be ascribed either to the virtue of the one or the vice of the other, seeing they were not yet born when the promise was given that "the older shall serve the younger".

Let it suffice us to hold fast what we gather from Paul's interpretation (Romans 9 v 10-13)—that whereas the whole human race deserves the same destruction, and is bound under the same sentence of condemnation, some are delivered by gracious mercy, others are justly left in their own destruction. And that those whom God has chosen are not preferred to others because God foresaw they *would* be holy, but in order that they *might* be holy. Among men some perish, some obtain salvation; but the cause of this depends on the secret will of God.

⊙ Apply

How do you react to the idea that God's will is the ultimate cause of our salvation?

Do you think that this gives us a license to behave as badly as Jacob often does in Genesis?

⊘ Pray

Praise God that he is sovereign in creation, revelation, redemption and final judgment.

Ask God to help you, as a Christian, to be in practice what he chose you to be (i.e. holy).

~ Notes and Prayers ~

Jacob's Ladder

Genesis 28 v 10-22

with John Calvin

C hrist is the mediator through whom all celestial blessings flow down to us and through whom we, in turn, ascend to God.

Read Genesis 28 v 10-22

What do you understand by the image of the ladder/stairway in Jacob's dream?

What is "the house of God ... the gate of heaven" (v 17)?

The Mediator

God manifested himself as seated upon a ladder which touched heaven and earth, and which was the vehicle of angels. To us who hold that the covenant of God was founded in Christ, and that Christ himself was the eternal image of the Father in which he manifested himself to the holy patriarchs, there is nothing in this vision intricate or ambiguous.

We are alienated from God by sin, and flee from his presence. Angels, to whom is committed the guardianship of the human race, do not communicate with us in such a way that we become conscious of their presence. It is Christ alone who connects heaven and earth: he is the only Mediator who reaches from heaven down to earth. Through him the fullness of all celestial blessings flows down to us; and we, in turn, ascend to God.

If, then, we say that the ladder is a figure of Christ, the exposition will not be forced. For the likeness of a ladder well suits the Mediator. We feel unspeakable joy when we hear that Christ, who so far excels all creatures, is nevertheless joined with us. His friendly and lovely image is depicted, that we may know by his descent that heaven is opened to us.

The Gate of Heaven

Jacob calls that place "the gate of heaven" (v 17). Because God is placed in heaven as on his royal throne, Jacob truly declares that in seeing God, he had penetrated into heaven. In this sense the preaching of the gospel is called the kingdom of heaven, and the sacraments may be called the gate of heaven, because they admit us into the presence of God.

Roman Catholics foolishly misapply this passage to their temples. But even if the places which they designate by this title ("House of God") were not polluted with ungodly superstitions, yet this honour belongs to no particular place, since Christ has filled the whole world with the presence of his deity. Only those helps to faith (preaching and the sacraments) by which God raises us to himself can be called the gates of heaven.

⊙ Apply

Do you think that Calvin is right to interpret the ladder as being a picture of Christ our mediator? (See also John 1 v 51.)

Do you think it is right to say that no particular place can now be called "the house of God"?

⊙ Pray

Praise and thank God for sending Jesus to be our Mediator.

Ask God to help you appreciate more the blessings of gospel preaching and gospel sacraments (baptism and the Lord's Supper).

~ Notes and Prayers ~

Day

38

Wrestling with God

Genesis 32 v 22-32

with John Calvin

The faithful become conquerors in their temptations only with the strength of God made perfect in their weakness, and by being injured and wounded in the conflict.

Read Genesis 32 v 22-32

Why do you think Jacob wrestled with this person?

Who do you think this person was?

Wrestling with Temptations

This vision taught Jacob that many conflicts awaited him, and that he would be the conqueror in them all. Yet there is not the least doubt that the Lord exhibited, in his person, a specimen of the temptations common to all his people which await them and must be constantly submitted to in this transitory life. So it is right to keep in view this design of the vision, which is to represent all the servants of God in this world as wrestlers, because the Lord exercises them with various kinds of conflicts.

Moreover, it is not said that Satan, or any mortal man, wrestled with Jacob, but God himself—to teach us that our faith is tried by him. Whenever we are tempted, our business is truly with him. For as all prosperity flows from his goodness, so adversity is either the rod with which he corrects our sins, or the test of our faith and patience.

We do not fight against him, except by his own power, and with his own weapons. For he, having challenged us to this contest, at the same time furnishes us with means of resistance, so that he both fights *against* us and *for* us.

God's Name

Jacob said, "Please tell me your name". Though his wish was pious, the Lord does not grant it, because the time of full revelation was not yet completed. For the fathers were required to walk in the twilight of morning, and the Lord manifested himself to them by degrees until, at length, Christ, the Sun of Righteousness, arose, in whom perfect brightness shines forth. Even Moses was only permitted to behold his glory from behind (Exodus 33 v 21-23); yet because he occupied an intermediate place between patriarchs and apostles, he is said to have seen "face to face" the God who had been hidden from the fathers (Exodus 33 v 11, Deuteronomy 34 v 10).

But now, since God has approached more nearly unto us, our ingratitude is most ungodly and detestable, if we do not run to meet him, with ardent desire to obtain such great grace.

⊘ Apply

How much do you actually wrestle with temptations and with God in prayer about them?

Why do you think God only "revealed himself by degrees" before Christ came?

⊘ Pray

Praise God that we can know him in Jesus, and one day will truly see him face to face.

Ask God to strengthen you in the battle with temptation, daily.

~ Notes and Prayers ~

Day

39

Joseph's Dreams

Genesis 37 v 1-11

with John Calvin

A s the hymn-writer William Cowper once put it, "God moves in a mysterious way, his wonders to perform"—in the life of Joseph, and of Christ.

Read Genesis 37 v 1-11

Why do you think God first revealed in a dream what would eventually happen in the story of Joseph?

Was it acceptable for the brothers to be jealous of and nasty towards Joseph?

They Hated Him

The brothers conceive enmity against Joseph, whom they see to be more tenderly loved by their father. That a many-coloured coat and similar trifles inflamed them to devise a scheme of slaughter is a proof of their detestable cruelty.

Having stated what were the first seeds of this enmity, Moses now ascends higher, and shows that Joseph had been elected, by the wonderful purpose of God, to great things. God revealed in dreams what he would do, that afterwards it might be known that nothing had happened by mere luck—it had been fixed by a celestial decree, which was in its proper time carried forward through circuitous windings to its completion.

God Protected Him

The sons of Jacob conspire to put to death the very person without whom they cannot be preserved. Indeed, he who was ordained to be the minister of salvation to them is thrown into a well, and with difficulty rescued from the jaws of death. Driven about by various misfortunes, he seems to be an alien from his father's house. Afterwards, he is cast into prison, as into another tomb, where, for a long time, he languishes. Nothing, therefore, was less probable than that the family of Jacob should be preserved by his means, when he was cut off from it, and carried far away, and not even reckoned among the living.

Nor did any hope of his liberation remain, especially from the time in which he was neglected by the chief butler. But being condemned to perpetual imprisonment, he was left there to rot. God, however, by such complicated methods, accomplishes what he had purposed.

In this history, we have not only a most beautiful example of divine providence, but also two other points are added especially worthy of notice: first, that the Lord performs his work by wonderful and unusual methods; and, secondly, that he brings forth the salvation of his church, not from magnificent splendour, but from death and the grave. In the person of Joseph, a lively image of Christ is presented.

⊙ Apply

Does thinking about how God worked in the life of Joseph and of Christ help you to trust him with the ups and downs of your own life?

What points of comparison and points of difference are there between Christ and Joseph?

⊙ Pray

Praise God for his providential guiding of history, and of our own lives.

Ask God to help you trust him, whether life is good at the moment for you, or not.

~ Notes and Prayers ~

Day
40

Joseph Flees Temptation

Genesis 39

with John Calvin

L et the faithful endeavour to live upright lives and prudently guard against every mark of evil, even if they must therefore endure the infamy of the world.

Read Genesis 39

Why was Joseph always so successful, wherever he ended up?

Why does he resist the temptation placed before him by Potiphar's wife?

God's Blessing

Let us learn, even amidst our sufferings, to perceive the grace of God. That grace shone forth in Joseph, in no common or usual manner. How base is our ingratitude if we do not refer all our prosperous events to God as their author, seeing that Scripture often teaches us that nothing proceeding from us, whether counsels, or labours, or any means which they can devise, will profit us, unless God gives his blessing.

We are also taught what an advantage it is to give hospitality to the elect children of God, or to join ourselves to those whom the divine favour thus accompanies, that it may spread its fragrance to those who are near them. But we ought above all to centre all our wishes on this one point, that God may be propitious to us.

Beauty and Integrity

We see here how many dangers those who excel in beauty are exposed to; for it is very difficult for them to restrain themselves from all lustful desires. Nothing is easier than for all our senses to infect our minds with depraved desires, unless we are very earnestly on our guard. For Satan never ceases diligently to suggest those things which may incite us to sin. So, let everyone endeavour carefully to govern their eyes, and their ears, and the other members of their body, unless they wish to open so many doors to Satan, into the innermost affections of their heart.

Joseph's constancy is commended. A real fear of God reigned in his mind. He chose to sacrifice his dignity, and was prepared to relinquish life itself, rather than to be guilty of wickedness before God. Seeing that the Spirit of God proposes to us such an example in a youth, what excuse does he leave for men and women of mature age, if they voluntarily throw themselves into sin, or fall into it by a light temptation?

May regard for God alone prevail to subdue all carnal affections. And may we more highly value a good and upright conscience than all the plaudits of the world.

⊘ Apply

Do you think your successes in this life are partly down to you and partly down to God's blessing?

How can you cultivate in advance the kind of integrity Joseph showed, so that if a crisis moment arises you are ready to respond in a godly way?

⊙ Pray

Thank God for all the blessings of this life which you enjoy, and give him all the credit for any recent successes.

Ask God to help you "control your own body in a way that is holy and honourable, not in passionate lust like the pagans, who do not know God" (1 Thessalonians 4 v 4-5).

~ Notes and Prayers ~

Day

41

God Meant It for Good

Genesis 50 v 15-21

with John Calvin

Whatever poison Satan produces, God turns it into medicine for his elect people. Let us adoringly rejoice in this mystery, even if it is beyond our comprehension.

Read Genesis 50 v 15-21

How has God turned the brothers' evil desires into good for his people (v 20)?

Does that mean that God sanctions evil?

Am I in Place of God?

Joseph considers the providence of God, and so imposes it on himself as a compulsory law, not only to grant pardon, but also to exercise generosity. Seeing that, by the secret counsel of God, he was led into Egypt for the purpose of preserving the life of his brethren, Joseph must devote himself to this object, lest he should resist God. In effect, he says, "Since God has deposited your life with me, I should be engaged in war against him, if I were not to be the faithful dispenser of the grace which he had committed to my hands".

You Meant to Harm Me

Joseph skilfully ascribes the government of all things to God, in a way that preserves the divine administration free from contracting any stain from our vices. The selling of Joseph was a crime detestable for its cruelty and treachery—yet he was not sold except by the decree of heaven. Thus we may say with truth and propriety that Joseph was sold by the wicked consent of his brethren, and by the secret providence of God. While they are contriving the destruction of their brother, God is effecting their deliverance from on high.

Yet it was not a work common to both, in the sense that God sanctioned anything connected with or relating to their wickedness. Nothing is done without God's will, because he governs human counsels, sways their wills, and regulates all events. But if people undertake anything right and just, he so actuates and moves them inwardly by his Spirit, that whatever is good in them may justly be said to come from him.

If Satan and the ungodly rage, he acts by their hands in such an inexpressible manner, that the wickedness and blame of the deed belongs to them alone. For they are not induced to sin, as the faithful are to act aright by the impulse of the Spirit—they are the authors of their own evil, and follow Satan as their leader. The justice of God shines brightly in the midst of the darkness of our sin.

⊘ Apply

What would you say to someone who said God was responsible for all the evil in the world, and for not sorting it out with his "supposedly" unlimited power?

Look back over the whole of Genesis; how has God transformed evil and turned it to good?

⊙ Pray

Praise God that he is in such control of the world that he can bring good out of evil without being contaminated by evil himself.

Ask God to help you trust his sovereign control and submit to his will, whether you can see how it's going to turn out or not.

~ Notes and Prayers ~

We Are Not Worthy

1 John 1 v 5-10

with John Harpsfield

W̵e learn from all good men in holy Scripture to humble ourselves, and to exalt, extol, praise, magnify and glorify God.

Read 1 John 1 v 5-10

What does John say about those who don't acknowledge their sin?

What is the best way to deal with sin, according to John?

Fruitless Trees

Few of the proud, just, learned, wise, perfect and holy Pharisees were saved by Jesus, because they justified themselves by their counterfeit holiness before people. Therefore, let us beware of such hypocrisy, vainglory and justifying of ourselves. Let us look at our feet, and then down peacock's feathers, down proud heart, down vile clay, frail and brittle vessels!

Of ourselves, we are crabtrees that can bring forth no apples. We are, of ourselves, of such earth, as can bring forth only weeds, nettles, brambles and briers. We have neither faith, love, hope, patience, chastity, nor any thing else that is good, except from God. And therefore, these virtues are called in Galatians 5, the fruit of the Holy Spirit, and not the fruit of mankind.

Imperfect and Unworthy

Let us, therefore, acknowledge ourselves before God to be miserable and wretched sinners. And let us earnestly repent, and humble ourselves heartily, and cry to God for mercy. Let us know our own works, how imperfect they are, and then we shall not stand foolishly and arrogantly in our own conceits, nor think we can be justi-fied by our merits or works.

For truly, there are imperfections in our best works. We do not love God as much as we are bound to do—with all our heart, mind and power. We do not fear God as much as we ought to do. We do not pray to God, but with great and many imperfec-tions. We give, forgive, believe, live and hope imperfectly. We speak, think and do imperfectly. We fight against the devil, the world and the flesh imperfectly. Let us, therefore, not be ashamed to confess plainly our state of imperfection. Indeed, let us not be ashamed to confess imperfection, even in all our own best works.

Let none of us be ashamed, to say with the apostle Peter, "I am a sinful man" (Luke 5 v 8). Let us all make open confession with the prodigal son to our father (Luke 15 v 18-19), and say with him, "Father, we have sinned against heaven and against you. We are not worthy to be called your children" .

⊙ Apply

How does it make you feel that, by nature, you are not "worthy" to be God's child?

What would you say to a non-Christian friend who says, "I do my best to live a good life—surely God will be happy with that"?

⊙ Pray

Ask forgiveness for the times when you have "followed too much the devices and desires of your own heart" (as the *Book of Common Prayer* puts it) this week.

Praise God that though we are more sinful than we could even imagine, he is more merciful than we could possibly dream.

~ Notes and Prayers ~

Day

43

I Believe

Deuteronomy 6 v 4-9 and Matthew 28 v 16-20

with Heinrich Bullinger

For the next two weeks we will be looking at Heinrich Bullinger's exposition of the Apostles' Creed (see page 139), a popular and influential Reformation work.

Read Deuteronomy 6 v 4-9 and Matthew 28 v 16-20

What do these two passages have in common?

What major differences can you spot?

I Believe in God

The first article of Christian faith is this: "I believe in God, the Father Almighty, Creator of heaven and earth". And this first article of the creed contains two points. For first, we say generally, "I believe in God". Then we descend particularly to the distinction of the persons and add "the Father Almighty". For God is one in substance, and three in persons. So understanding the unity of the substance, we say plainly, "I believe in God". And again, keeping and not confounding the persons we add, "in the Father Almighty... in Jesus Christ his only Son... and in the Holy Spirit".

Let us therefore believe that God is one, not many, and pure in substance; but three in persons—the Father, the Son, and the Holy Spirit. For in the Law it is written, "Hear, O Israel: The LORD our God, the LORD is one". And again, in the Gospel we read that the Lord said, "[baptise] them in the name of the Father and of the Son and of the Holy Spirit".

Not "We" But "I"

By the way, we should particularly note this, that when we pray we say, "Our Father in heaven ... give us today our daily bread". But when we confess our faith, we do not say "We believe", but "I believe". For faith is required of every one of us, for every particular person to have without deceit in their heart, and without double meaning to profess it with their mouth. It was not enough for Abraham to have faith for all his offspring. Neither will it be of any use to you for another person to believe if you yourself are without faith.

God is the object and foundation of our faith, the everlasting and chief goodness, never weary but always ready to help us. We therefore believe in God, that is to say, we put our whole hope, all our safety, and ourselves wholly into his hands, since he is able to preserve and bestow on us all things that are necessary for our benefit.

⊙ Apply

Do you tend to think of God as "one substance" or as "three persons"? How can you hold those together as the Bible does?

Do you yourself hope and trust in this God, or are you relying on someone else to do your believing for you?

⊙ Pray

Praise God that he not only created us but also revealed himself to us in his word so that we could be friends with him.

Ask God to give you first-hand faith, not second-hand faith, to trust in him.

~ Notes and Prayers ~

~ The Apostles' Creed ~

I believe in God, the Father Almighty,
Creator of heaven and earth.

I believe in Jesus Christ,
his only Son our Lord.
He was conceived by the Holy Spirit
and born of the virgin Mary.
He suffered under Pontius Pilate,
was crucified, died, and was buried.
He descended to the dead.
On the third day he rose again.

He ascended into heaven,
and sits at the right hand of the Father.
From there he shall come again to
judge the living and the dead.

I believe in the Holy Spirit,
the holy catholic church,
the communion of saints,
the forgiveness of sins,
the resurrection of the body,
and the life everlasting. Amen.

I Believe
in Jesus Christ

Hebrews 1 v 1-4

with Heinrich Bullinger

The second article of the Apostles' Creed is about Jesus Christ, our Lord, the Son of God, in whom we put our whole hope and confidence for life and salvation.

Read Hebrews 1 v 1-4

To whom is the Son superior (v 1 and 4)?

Who is he and what has he done?

The Only Son of God

There are three things we should note about the Son of God, in whom we believe. First, that he is called the only Son. If he is the Son of God, then his nature and substance is a divine nature and substance. For the writer of Hebrews calls him, "The radiance of the glory of God and the exact imprint of his nature" (Hebrews 1 v 3). Quite rightly, therefore, do the holy fathers say that the Son is of the same substance and being with the Father.

We also are called sons of God, but not by participation of nature, or likeness of substance, or naturally, but by adoption. And this is why the Jews were offended when he called himself the Son of God, because they perceived that he was claiming to be the natural Son of God, equal to God, and God himself (John 5 v 18; 10 v 30-33).

These are most evident testimonies of the natural Godhead of Christ. And unless the Son was God by nature, he could not be the Saviour of the world.

Jesus Christ

Secondly, this Son is called Jesus Christ. The name Jesus was given to him by God's appointment from heaven, the angel instructing Joseph, saying, "You are to give him the name Jesus, because he will save his people from their sins" (Matthew 1 v 21).

He is also called *Christ*, which means "anointed". The Jews call him *Messiah*, a title for a king or priest, for they of old anointed their kings and priests with oil. But the true Christ was anointed with the very true ointment, that is, with the fullness of the Holy Spirit.

Our Lord

Thirdly, he is also called "our Lord", for two reasons. First, with respect to the mystery of our redemption. For Christ is the Lord of all the elect, whom he has delivered from the power and dominion of Satan, sin and death, and made them a people for his own possession. Christ is also called Lord in respect of his divine power and nature, by which all things are in subjection to him.

⊙ Apply

Marvel at the depth of the simple statement in the creed: "I believe in Jesus Christ, God's only Son our Lord."

Do you really believe he is the divine Son, our anointed Saviour and true King?

⊙ Pray

Ask God to help you bow down to Jesus as your Lord and God.

Praise God for sending Jesus to save us from our sins.

~ Notes and Prayers ~

Day
45

Conceived by the Spirit Born of the Virgin

Luke 1 v 26-35

with Heinrich Bullinger

The chief cause of Christ's incarnation is to be a mediator between God and us, and by intercession to join or bring into one those who were severed.

Read Luke 1 v 26-35

What does the angel say to Mary about the child to be born (v 31-35)?

Why does the angel mention King David, who had been dead for 1000 years?

The Conception of Christ

In this third article of the Creed, I have to declare how Jesus came into the world: that is, by incarnation. This article contains two things: the conception of Christ, and his birth.

He was conceived by the Holy Spirit. All humans, except Christ, are conceived by the seed of man, which is of itself unclean, and therefore we are born sinners. But the body of Christ our Lord was not conceived in the Virgin Mary by Joseph, but by the Holy Spirit. By his eternal power, she conceived of her own blood and gave a pure and truly human body to the Son of God.

God himself, straight after the very beginning of the world, foretold this. For he did not say the offspring of the man would bruise the serpent's head, but "the seed of the woman" (Genesis 3 v 15).

Because she was a daughter of King David's stock, and because, God so working, she of her own substance gave substance to the Son of God, her child is also called the son of David. He could not be called David's son unless he had taken true human substance from Mary, a maid or daughter of the line of David.

The Virgin Birth

Moreover, his birth is pure. For he was born of the virgin so that she was both a mother and a virgin. For Isaiah says, "The virgin will conceive and give birth to a son" (Isaiah 7 v 14).

So as the apostle John says, "The Word became flesh" (John 1 v 14). And the writer of Hebrews says that the Lord was "made like them, fully human in every way", sin excepted (Hebrews 2 v 16-17). To the Philippians, the apostle Paul says, "who, being in very nature God, did not consider equality with God something to be used to his own advantage; rather, he made himself nothing by taking the very nature of a servant, being made in human likeness. And being found in appearance as a man..." (Philippians 2 v 6-8).

Let us therefore confess that Jesus Christ was conceived by the Holy Spirit, and born of the virgin Mary.

⊙ Apply

Rejoice that God prophesied and fulfilled the amazing incarnation of his Son, for us and for our salvation.

What would you say to someone who said it doesn't matter if Jesus got his human nature from Mary through a virgin birth, or whether the virgin birth is true or not?

⊙ Pray

Praise God the Father for sending Jesus, his Son, to empty himself and be born as a man, to crush the serpent's head.

Ask God to help you grasp the depths of Jesus' humility, and show that humility in your relationships with others.

~ Notes and Prayers ~

The Passion of Christ

Isaiah 53 v 1-6

with Heinrich Bullinger

The Son of God became incarnate in order to make a sacrifice to appease God's justice and to purge away our sins in his own body.

Read Isaiah 53 v 1-6

What kinds of suffering did the person described here go through?

For whom did he endure all this?

He Suffered under Pontius Pilate

This article of the Creed declares the purpose and use of the Lord's incarnation. For he became man that he might suffer and die, and by dying and suffering might redeem us from eternal death and the torments of hell, and make us (being once cleansed) heirs of everlasting life.

We confess that our Lord truly suffered and not just to the appearance only; and that he truly suffered the calamities and miseries of this world and, after that, the torments of the slaughtermen, and death itself in most bitter pangs. He suffered therefore both in soul and body, in many ways. But truly he suffered all this for us, for in him was neither sin nor any other cause why he should suffer.

We do expressly declare the manner of his death, for we add, "he was crucified and died on the cross". But the death of the cross, as it was most shameful, so also was it most bitter or sharp to be suffered. Yet he took that kind of death upon him, that he might make satisfaction for the world, and fulfil that which from the beginning was prefigured.

The Fruit of His Death

What is the fruit of Christ's death? First we were accursed because of sin; he therefore took our curse upon himself, being lifted up upon the cross, so that he might take our curse away, and that we might be blessed in him.

The inheritance bequeathed to us by his "will and testament" could not come to us unless he which bequeathed it did die (Hebrews 9 v 15-17). But God bequeathed it, and so that he might be able to die, he became man and died according to his human nature. He did this so that we might receive the inheritance of life.

Paul says, "God made him who had no sin to be sin for us, so that in him we might become the righteousness of God" (2 Corinthians 5 v 21). Our Lord therefore became man, by the sacrifice of himself to make satisfaction for us.

⊙ Apply

Read through Isaiah 53 v 4-6 again, putting your own name, or "my" instead of "our", to appreciate all that Christ did for you.

Count up all the different aspects of the cross which are discussed here—do you understand what they all mean? If not, how will you find out more?

⊙ Pray

Praise God for what Christ has done in your place.

Ask God to help you understand more about the fruit of the cross.

~ Notes and Prayers ~

Day
47

He Rose Again

1 Corinthians 15 v 12-19

with Heinrich Bullinger

The resurrection of our Lord Jesus Christ certifies and assures us of our salvation and redemption, so that we can no longer doubt it.

Read 1 Corinthians 15 v 12-19

Would it be so bad if Jesus had not physically come back from the dead?

Is the resurrection just a pious belief to help us through this life?

Death Defeated

The fifth article of our creed is, "On the third day he rose again from the dead". And this article is in a way the chief of all the rest. Neither are the apostles so busily occupied in declaring and confirming the others, as they are this one. For it would not have been enough if our Lord had simply died, unless he had also risen again from the dead.

For if he had not risen from the dead, but had remained still in death, who should have persuaded us that sin was purged by the death of Christ, that death was vanquished, and Satan overcome? Indeed, we have foolish fellows who would never cease to blaspheme God himself, to make a mock of our hope, and to say, "Tush! Who ever returned from the dead, to tell us whether there is life in another world after this one or not, and what kind of life it is?"

That the Lord therefore might declare to the whole world that after this life there is another, and that the soul does not die with the body but remains alive, he returned to his disciples on the third day alive again. And at that instant he showed them that sin was purged, death disarmed, and the devil vanquished.

The Devil Vanquished

The sting of death is sin. The reward of sin is death. The devil has the power of death, and shuts people up in hell for sin. Now, however, since Christ rose alive again from the dead, death could have no dominion over him. And because death, by suffering the Lord to pass through it, is broken, it must follow that the devil and hell are vanquished by Christ. And, lastly, that sin—the strength and power of them all—is purely purged.

The resurrection of our Lord Jesus Christ certifies and assures us of our salvation and redemption, so that we can no longer doubt of it. We confess, therefore, in this article, that our Lord Jesus Christ is risen again, and that he is risen again for our benefit.

⊙ Apply

Rejoice that Jesus really did rise again on the third day to give us true and solid hope.

Ponder the fact that the resurrection of Jesus was not just for his benefit, but for ours.

⊙ Pray

Thank God not just for sending Jesus to die in our place, but also to live again for us.

Ask God to help you trust him more for that future life beyond death, and to live in the light of it.

~ Notes and Prayers ~

He Ascended into Heaven

Hebrews 10 v 11-14

with Heinrich Bullinger

J esus is seated at the right hand of the Father, resting happily from his labours, yet not idly leaning on his elbows but continuing to do the work of our Priest and King.

Read Hebrews 10 v 11-14

What are the contrasts between Old Testament priests and Jesus, our great High Priest?

Why is it important for us that Jesus ascended into heaven and is seated at the right hand of the Father?

The Risen and Ascended Lord

The sixth article of our faith is that Christ ascended into heaven, and sits at the right hand of God the Father Almighty. That body which is of the same substance with our bodies, taken out of the virgin Mary, and taken truly of the substance of the virgin, which hung upon the cross and died and was buried and rose again—the very same body I say, ascended into the heavens, and sits at the right hand of God the Father. For after forty days, our Lord had instructed his disciples abundantly enough touching the truth of his resurrection and the kingdom of God (Acts 1 v 1-3).

By that ascension of his, he declares to the whole earth that he is Lord of all things, and that to him are subject all things in heaven and on earth. The ascension declares that he is our strength, the power of the faithful. For he, ascending into heaven, has lead captivity itself captive (Ephesians 4 v 8), and by plundering his enemies has enriched his people, on whom he daily heaps his spiritual gifts.

His Body Is in Heaven

Furthermore, he ascended into heaven to the end that we might be assuredly certified of eternal salvation by this. For by ascending he prepared a place for us; he made ready the way; that is, he opened the very heavens to the faithful.

Christ our Lord, with respect to his divinity, is not shut up in any place; but according to his humanity, he is in the very specific location of heaven. In the meantime, he is not here on earth or everywhere bodily, but being separated from us in body, he remains in heaven—for he ascended. As Augustine said truly, "In terms of his actual body, Christ our Lord is in some one place of heaven".

He is taken, I say, into the place appointed for those that are saved. For Paul the apostle speaking plainly enough to be understood says, "But our citizenship is in heaven. And we eagerly await a Saviour from there, the Lord Jesus Christ" (Philippians 3 v 20).

⊙ Apply

If it is good to have "friends in high places", how much better is it to have our Lord and Saviour there?

Would it matter if Jesus' body was not limited to being in one place at a time? Would it matter if his body was not located in heaven until he comes again?

⊙ Pray

Rejoice that our Saviour is in heaven, having completed his work for us.

Ask Jesus to continue "heaping on" the church all the spiritual gifts it needs to serve him.

~ Notes and Prayers ~

Day
49

In Christ
Alone

Ephesians 2 v 1-5

with Thomas Cranmer

As of ourselves comes all evil and damnation, so likewise of God alone comes all goodness and salvation.

Read Ephesians 2 v 1-5

Who did we follow and obey, when we were dead in our sins (v 2-3)?

Why did God make us alive and save us (v 4-5)?

No Glory or Rejoicing in Ourselves

We have heard how evil we are of ourselves, and how of ourselves and by ourselves we have no goodness, help, or salvation—but rather, on the contrary, sin, damnation, and death everlasting. If we deeply weigh and consider this, we shall better understand the great mercy of God, and how our salvation comes only by Christ.

For in ourselves we find nothing by which we may be delivered from this miserable captivity into which we were cast, through the envy of the devil, by transgressing God's commandment in our first parent Adam. We have all become unclean, but we all are not able to cleanse ourselves, nor to make each other clean. We are by nature children of God's wrath, but we are not able to make ourselves the children and inheritors of God's glory. We are sheep that have gone astray, but we cannot of our own power come again to the sheepfold, so great is our imperfection and weakness.

We may not glory in ourselves, therefore, since of ourselves we are nothing but sinful. Neither may we rejoice in any works that we do, which are all so imperfect and impure that they are not able to stand before the righteous throne of God. As the holy prophet David says, "Do not bring your servant into judgment, for no one living is righteous before you" (Psalm 143 v 2).

Rejoice in Christ Alone

To God, therefore, we must flee, or else we shall never find peace, rest and quietness of conscience in our hearts. For he is the Father of mercies, and God of all consolation.

O how much are we bound to our heavenly Father, for his great mercies, which he has so plenteously declared to us in Christ Jesus our Lord and Saviour! What thanks worthy and sufficient can we give to him? Let us all with one accord burst out with joyful voices, ever praising and magnifying this Lord of mercy for his tender kindness shown to us in his dearly beloved Son!

⊙ Apply

Let us learn to know ourselves, our frailty and weakness, without any ostentation or boasting of our own good deeds and merits.

Let us also acknowledge the exceedingly great mercy of God towards us, which we don't deserve.

⊙ Pray

Confess to God how you have left undone those things which you ought to have done, and done those things which you ought not to have done.

Praise him for his mercy and grace towards you in Christ, despite your sin.

~ Notes and Prayers ~

Day

50

Jesus
the Judge

2 Thessalonians 1 v 5-12

with Heinrich Bullinger

We believe that our Lord Jesus Christ, on Judgment Day, shall deliver all the godly, and destroy all the wicked as he has said.

Read 2 Thessalonians 1 v 5-12

How will Judgment Day be different for those who don't believe and those who do?

How does Paul pray for believers, in the light of the coming Judgment Day?

Grace and Justice

The seventh article of our faith is this: "From heaven he shall come again to judge the living and the dead". In the former articles of the Apostles' Creed there is set forth and confessed the divine goodness, bountifulness, and grace in Christ. Now also shall be declared the divine justice, severity, and vengeance that is in him.

For there are two comings of our Lord Jesus Christ. First, he came humbly in the flesh to be the Redeemer and Saviour of the world. At the second time he shall come gloriously to be a Judge and implacable avenger against all unrepentant sinners and evildoers. He shall come out of heaven from the right hand of the Father in his visible and truly human body, to be seen by everyone, with the incomprehensible power of his Godhead and being attended on by all the angels.

The Sheep and the Goats

Then, the sheep shall be caught up into the clouds to meet the Lord in the air, and shall ascend with him joyfully into heaven to the right hand of God the Father, there to live for ever in glory and gladness (Matthew 25 v 31-46). But the bottom of the earth shall gape open for the wicked and shall suck them all up horribly, and send them down to hell. There, they shall be tormented for ever with Satan and his angels. All this shall be done not by any long, troublesome, or changeable process as is used in our courts of law, but in the twinkling of an eye. For then shall everyone's hearts be laid open and everyone's own conscience shall accuse them.

We confess therefore in this seventh article that we believe there shall be an end of all things in this world, and that the happiness of the wicked shall not continue for ever. For we believe that God is a just God, who has given all judgment to his Son (John 5 v 22), to repay to everyone in that day according to their works: pains to the wicked that never shall be ended and, to the godly, joys everlasting.

⊙ Apply

What would you say to someone who thought God was less fair than a human judge?

Why is it important that there is an end to the happiness of the wicked in this world?

⊙ Pray

Pray that by his grace God would give you faith to trust in him on that day, and to make you worthy of his calling.

Pray for those who do not (yet) know Jesus, that they would repent and believe in him before it is too late.

~ Notes and Prayers ~

Day
51

The Sanctifier

1 Corinthians 6 v 9-11

with Heinrich Bullinger

C hrist pours into us his Holy Spirit—the fullness of all good things—and communicates himself to us, joining us to himself with an unbreakable knot.

Read 1 Corinthians 6 v 9-11

What is the difference between what we were *and what we are* in Christ?

What part does the Holy Spirit play in our salvation (v 11)?

The Seal of the Spirit

The eighth article of our belief is this: "I believe in the Holy Spirit". This third part of the Creed contains the nature of the third person in the Holy Trinity. And we do rightly believe in the Holy Spirit, as well as in the Father and the Son. For the Holy Spirit is one God with the Father and the Son. And rightly is faith in the Holy Spirit joined to faith in the Father and the Son. For by him the fruit of God's salvation, fulfilled in the Son, is sealed to us. Our sanctification and cleansing is bestowed on us and derived from him to us by the Holy Spirit.

For the apostle says, "[God] anointed us, set his seal of ownership on us, and put his Spirit in our hearts as a deposit, guaranteeing what is to come" (2 Corinthians 1 v 21-22). And again, you were indeed once defiled, "But you were washed, you were sanctified, you were justified in the name of the Lord Jesus Christ and by the Spirit of our God" (1 Corinthians 6 v 11).

The Spirit and Sanctification

The Father indeed does sanctify too, but by the blood of Jesus Christ, and he pours the same sanctification out of him into us by the Holy Spirit. So it is, as it were, the property of the Holy Spirit to sanctify, which is why he is called Holy or the Sanctifier. Therefore, as often as we hear the Holy Spirit named, we must think of the power which Scripture attributes to him, and we must look to the benefits that flow from him to us.

In this eighth article we profess that we truly believe that all the faithful are cleansed, washed, regenerated, sanctified, enlightened, and enriched by God with diverse gifts of grace for Christ's sake, but yet through the Holy Spirit. For without him there is no true sanctification. Therefore, we ought not to attribute these gifts of grace to any other means—this glory belongs to the Holy Spirit only.

⊙ Apply

Do you tend to think of the Holy Spirit as an impersonal force, or as a divine person who is intimately involved in your salvation?

What would you say to someone who called the Holy Spirit "the forgotten person of the Trinity"?

⊙ Pray

Praise God the Father, God the Son, and God the Holy Spirit for all they have done to save and sanctify you.

Ask God to continue working in you, to change you to be more like Jesus.

~ Notes and Prayers ~

○
Day
52

The Church

Ephesians 1 v 3-14

with Heinrich Bullinger

W e must acknowledge and confess the holy catholic (universal) church, but not believe *in* the holy catholic church in the same way we believe in God the Holy Trinity.

Read Ephesians 1 v 3-14

Was the church chosen because it was holy?

How are heaven and earth united in Christ, do you think (v 10)?

The Holy Catholic Church

The church is an assembly, where the people are called out or gathered together. It is the company, communion, congregation, multitude, or fellowship of all who profess the name of Christ.

It is called "catholic" because this fellowship is universal, extended throughout all places and ages. For the true church of Christ is not limited to some corner: it stretches out through the compass of the world and into every age, containing all the faithful from the first Adam even to the very last saint who shall remain before the end of the world.

This universal church has her particular churches—I mean the church of Adam and of the Patriarchs, the church of Moses and of the Prophets before the birth of Christ, the Christian church named of Christ himself, and the apostolical church gathered together by the apostles' doctrine in the name of Christ. And it contains particular churches—such as the church of Jerusalem, of Antioch, of Alexandria, of Rome, of Asia, of Africa, of Europe, of the East, of the West, etc. And yet all these churches are members of one body under the only head, Christ. For Christ alone is the head of his church, not only that which is triumphant in heaven, but also that which is "militant" (battling evil) on earth.

The Communion of Saints

Between God and us there is a communion, that is, a fellowship and participation, a sharing between us of all good and heavenly things. By "the communion of saints" we also understand that we are fellows and partakers with all the saints (either living in heaven or on earth). For we are members together with them under one head, Christ.

But who can worthily set forth the great goodness of God's gift? What could be more delightful to our ears than to hear that all the saints, in heaven as well as on earth, are our brethren, and that we are members, partners, and fellows with them? Blessed be God who has so liberally bestowed his blessing on us in Christ his Son!

⊙ Apply

What would you say to someone who said we have nothing in common with Christians from another part of the world or another part of history?

What difference does it make to think of yourself as part of the history-spanning, global church of Christ, rather than just a member of a local congregation?

⊙ Pray

Thank God for making you a part of something which extends throughout time and space.

Ask him to help you understand the depths of what it means to be part of his church.

~ Notes and Prayers ~

Day

53

Forgiveness

Matthew 6 v 9-14

with Heinrich Bullinger

It is assuredly true that by the death of Christ, those who believe have all their sins forgiven, without having to go to confession or somehow make payment to God.

Read Matthew 6 v 9-14

Why do you think sins are spoken of in some versions of the Lord's Prayer as "debts"?

Do you think we need to pray this prayer more than once?

Forgive Us Our Debts

First, we must acknowledge and confess that we are sinners, and that by nature we are the children of wrath and damnation. For John does not in vain nor without a cause call everyone a liar who says they have no sin (1 John 1 v 8). And God, who knows our hearts, has commanded us, even until the last gasp, to pray saying, "Forgive us our debts".

Secondly, let us believe that all these sins of ours are pardoned and forgiven by God, not because we acknowledge and confess them, but because of the merit and blood of the Son of God—not for our own works or merits, but for the truth and mercy or grace of God. For we plainly profess, saying, "I believe in the forgiveness of sins". We don't say, "I buy, or by gifts do get, or by works obtain the forgiveness of sins," but "I believe in the forgiveness of sins".

The word "remission" or "forgiveness" means a free pardoning, by a metaphor taken from the world of creditors and debtors. So in respect of us, who do not have the ability to repay, our sins are freely forgiven. But in respect of God's justice, they are forgiven for the merit and satisfaction of Christ.

The Devil's Net

The Lord alone forgives sins. It is enough for us to confess our sins to God. Because he sees our hearts, he therefore is the most appropriate one to hear our confessions.

The Lord does not impute our sins to us, to our damnation; though sin itself remains in us, as a sting in the flesh. So we need to remove from the flesh the nourishment of evil and pray often, calling out to God for aid, so we are not overcome by evil. And if anyone happens to fail, out of their feebleness, and is subdued by temptation, let them not yield by lying still, to be caught in the devil's net. Let them rise up again by repentance, and run to Christ, believing that by the death of Christ this fall shall be forgiven.

⊘ Apply

Do you believe deep down that your debts are freely forgiven, or do you sometimes think that you still need to pay God back?

When caught in the devil's net, do you repent and run to Christ, or freeze in your failure?

⊙ Pray

Ask God to forgive your sins, as you forgive those who sin against you.

Praise God that he does not credit our sins to our account, but forgives us because of Jesus' death in our place.

~ Notes and Prayers ~

Day

54

Our Resurrection

1 Corinthians 15 v 50-58

with Heinrich Bullinger

By God's almighty power, our souls will return out of heaven, every one to its own body, so that the whole, perfect and full person may live for ever both in soul and body.

Read 1 Corinthians 15 v 50-58

What kind of change should we expect when we are raised again?

What will be missing or gone after that transformation?

Body and Soul

The eleventh article of the Apostles' Creed is the resurrection of the body. This article and the twelfth summarise as briefly as possible the most excellent fruit of faith, and sum of all perfection. They wrap up the end of faith in confessing life everlasting and the full and perfect salvation of the whole person.

For the whole person shall be saved, both soul and body. For since by sin we perished both in body and soul, so ought we to be restored again both bodily and spiritually. The soul is a spirit and does not die at all; but the body is earthly and therefore does die and rot. Because of this, many hold the opinion that our bodies die, never to be made partakers of joy or pain in the world to come. But we profess the opposite, acknowledging that our bodies shall rise again and enter into life everlasting. Let us therefore believe that our bodies, which are taken of the earth and turn into dust and ashes, are quickened and live again.

We Will Be Like Jesus

Did not Christ himself, having once broken the tyranny of death, rise up again on the third day? Did he not rise again in the same substance of flesh in which he had hung on the cross and been buried? Not without good cause do we look back to Christ, "the firstborn from among the dead" (Colossians 1 v 18), when we think about the manner of our own resurrection. For the members shall rise again in the same way in which the head is risen up before them. We, it is true, shall not rise again "on the third day" after our death, but we too shall rise at the last day in the very same body in which we now live.

For our Lord's body after his resurrection was neither turned into a ghost nor brought to nothing nor incapable of being recognised. For he showed them his hands and feet, easily known by the imprint of the nails which had crucified him, and said, "It is I" (Luke 24 v 36-43).

⊘ Apply

What difference does it make to know that in eternity we will not just be souls but body and soul?

How does it make you feel that Jesus "will transform our lowly bodies so that they will be like his glorious body" (Philippians 3 v 21)?

⊘ Pray

Praise God that he cares for every part of us, both body and soul.

Thank God that on resurrection day we will be changed and rise with imperishable, incorruptible, sinless immortality.

~ Notes and Prayers ~

Day
55

Everlasting Life

1 Thessalonians 4 v 13-18

with Heinrich Bullinger

The joys of heaven differ a great deal from the joys of earth, and they will continue for ever into eternity.

Read 1 Thessalonians 4 v 13-18

What happens to those who die before Christ returns again in glory?

What is the end point that Christians are all heading towards?

Immediate Transformation

Through the Apostles' Creed we say, "I believe that I shall live for ever both in body and soul, and that everlastingness is truly perpetual and has no end". Moreover, our souls are made partakers of this eternal life immediately after they depart out of our bodies, as the Lord himself witnesses, saying, "Whoever hears my word and believes him who sent me has eternal life and will not be judged but has crossed over from death to life" (John 5 v 24).

Our bodies are buried and putrefy, but they shall at length be received into eternal life when, being raised up, they shall after the time of judgment be caught into the air, there to meet Christ, that they may be for ever with the Lord. For then our souls return out of heaven, every one to its own body, that the whole, perfect and full person may live for ever both in soul and body. As eternal life came to the head, Christ, so shall it also come to every member of Christ.

Seeing and Enjoying God

Scripture, with eloquent and figurative speeches, with allusions and enigmatic sentences, most plainly shows the shadow of that life and those joys. Yet all that is little or nothing in comparison to what we shall see when that day arrives, and we shall with unspeakable joy behold God himself, the creator of all things in his glory, Christ our Saviour in his majesty, and all the blessed souls, angels, patriarchs, prophets, apostles, martyrs, our fathers—all the host of heaven—and lastly the whole divine and heavenly glory.

To be short, we shall see God face to face; we shall be filled with the company of God, and yet be never weary of him. And the face of God is not that countenance which appears in us, but is a most delectable revealing and enjoying of God, which no mortal tongue can worthily declare.

Let us so believe and live that when we depart from this life, we may experience those unspeakable joys of the eternal life to come, which now we do believe.

⊙ Apply

What do you look forward to most about the life to come?

Are you eager to enjoy the "delectable revealing" of God's face?

⊙ Pray

Thank God that there are such unspeakable joys to look forward to in glory.

Ask him to strengthen you to believe in these things to come, and live in the light of them.

~ Notes and Prayers ~

Day
56

The Wrath of God Was Satisfied

Romans 3 v 21-26

with Thomas Cranmer

Although justification is by faith alone and free to us, yet it was not achieved without the payment of a ransom.

Read Romans 3 v 21-26

What did God do to enable us to be redeemed, despite our sin?

How can it be right for God to say that I'm in the right when I'm not?

Making Amends for Us

No one can by their own acts, works and deeds be justified, and made righteous before God. But everyone of necessity is constrained to seek for another righteousness, or justification, to be received at God's own hands—that is to say, the remission, pardon, and forgiveness of sins and trespasses, in such things as we have offended.

And this justification or righteousness, which we so receive by God's mercy and Christ's merits, embraced by faith, is taken, accepted and allowed of God, for our perfect and full justification. It is our duty ever to remember the great mercy of God, how (all the world being wrapped in sin, by breaking of the law) God sent his only Son, our Saviour Christ into this world, to fulfil the law for us; and by shedding of his most precious blood, to make a sacrifice and satisfaction or to make amends to his Father for our sins—to satisfy his wrath and indignation conceived against us because of them.

Justice and Mercy Embrace

In this mystery of our redemption, by the great wisdom of God, he has so tempered his justice and mercy together that he would neither by his justice condemn us unto the perpetual captivity of the devil and his prison of hell—remediless for ever without mercy—nor by his mercy deliver us clearly without justice, or payment of a just ransom. But with his endless mercy, he joined his most upright and equal justice.

His great mercy he showed to us in delivering us from our former captivity, without requiring any ransom to be paid or amends to be made on our part—which it would have been impossible for us to do. And since we did not have it in us to do so, he provided a ransom for us—the most precious body and blood of his own most dear and best beloved Son, Jesus Christ, who besides his ransom, fulfilled the law for us perfectly. And so the justice of God and his mercy did embrace together, and fulfilled the mystery of our redemption.

⊘ Apply

When you rejoice in the fact that salvation is by grace alone, never forget that what is freely given to us was bought with the precious blood of Christ.

Remember that God did not indulgently set aside his justice in order to save us, but fulfilled it.

⊙ Pray

Rejoice that Jesus bore the wrath of God for our sins, so that we don't have to.

Thank God that he is not merely the God of perfect justice, but also the God of endless mercy.

~ Notes and Prayers ~

Loving God
and Neighbour

Luke 10 v 25-37

with Heinrich Bullinger

As we begin now to explore the Ten Commandments (Exodus 20 v 1-17), Bullinger teaches that God's love works in us to make us want to obey the one we heartily love, and also to love our neighbour as ourselves.

Read Luke 10 v 25-37

How much should we love God?

Who is our neighbour?

Love God

Love is a gift given to us from heaven by which we love God with our hearts before and above all things, and our neighbour as ourselves.

Love therefore springs from heaven, from where it is poured into our hearts. But it is enlarged and augmented partly by the remembrance and consideration of God's benefits, partly by regular prayer, and also by hearing the word of Christ. Which things themselves are also the gifts of the Spirit. For truly the love of God, by which he loves us, is the foundation and cause of our love for him.

We must love God entirely, and cleave to him as the only chief and eternal goodness. In him we delight ourselves and are well pleased, and frame ourselves to his will and pleasure.

Indeed, it is pleasant and sweet to those who heartily love God to do the things which they perceive are acceptable to God. Their only joy is, as often as possible, to talk with God and to hear the words of God speaking in Scripture.

Love Your Neighbour

We must also love our neighbour as ourselves. But who is our neighbour? There are some who think that their kinsfolk are their neighbours. Others consider their benefactors to be their neighbours, and judge that those who do them harm are strangers. But our Lord Jesus Christ tells us that everyone, even if they are our enemy, is nevertheless our neighbour, if they stand in need of our aid or counsel.

The Lord speaks in the Gospel about love for our neighbours when he says, "Love your enemies, do good to those who hate you, bless those who curse you, pray for those who ill-treat you" (Luke 6 v 27-28). And again, "Give to everyone who asks you ... If you love those who love you, what credit is that to you? Even sinners love those who love them" (Luke 6 v 30, 32). So then, everyone who stands in need of our aid both is, and is to be counted, our neighbour.

⊙ Apply

Is it "pleasant and sweet" for you to obey God, even when he says things you find hard?

Are there people you find it especially difficult to love in the way God wants you to?

⊙ Pray

Ask God to help you love him with all your heart, all your soul, all your mind and all your strength.

Ask God to help you love your neighbour as yourself, even when you don't like them.

~ Notes and Prayers ~

The Uses
of the Law

Psalm 19 v 7-14

with Heinrich Bullinger

The use of the law of God can be said to be threefold: revealing our sin,
teaching us the way, and restraining the ungodly.

Read Psalm 19 v 7-14

What good is the law of the Lord, according to David, the writer of this psalm?

What effect does the law have, when he thinks about himself in its light?

The Law Reveals Our Sin

The use of God's law is manifold, and yet it may be reduced to three particular points.

The chief and proper office of the law is to convince everyone that they are guilty
of sin. For the law of God sets forth to us the holy will of God, and in doing so it
requires of us a most perfect and absolute kind of righteousness. Which of us
fulfils all the points of the law? Which of us has ever had a pure heart within us?
Who ever loved God with all their heart, with all their soul, and with all their mind?

Therefore the law is a kind of looking-glass in which we behold our own corruption, frailty, stupidity, imperfection, and our judgment—that is, our just and deserved condemnation. Therefore the law also sets forth the true doctrine of justification, teaching plainly that we are justified by faith in Christ, and not by the merits
of our own works.

The Law Teaches Us the Way

The second use of the law is to teach those who are justified by faith in Christ what to do and what not to do. We must acknowledge that all the forms of virtues, and the treasure of all goodness, is presented to us in the law of the Lord.

The first of the two tables of the moral law *(the first group of four commandments)* teaches us what we owe to God and how he wants to be worshipped. The second table frames our lives and teaches us how to behave towards our neighbour.

The Law Restrains the Ungodly

The third use of the law is to repress the unruly. Those who cannot be moved to orderliness by reason are constrained by punishment so that honesty, peace and public tranquillity may be maintained.

It is impossible for anyone of their own strength to fulfil the law and fully satisfy the will of God in all points. But whatever is promised and prefigured in the law— all those things, Christ our Lord has fulfilled.

⊙ Apply

Think about a time when being told a rule made you suddenly want to break it.

Ponder how people you know have house rules which help you to know how to make them happy.

⊙ Pray

Praise the Lord Jesus that he perfectly kept the law in every point, on our behalf.

Ask God to strengthen and enlighten you to understand and keep his law.

~ Notes and Prayers ~

Day
59

No Other Gods but Me

Exodus 19 v 1-6 and 20 v 1-7

with Heinrich Bullinger

Let God alone be our God—that is, our life, our safeguard, our help and refuge, our protection and deliverance, our hope and love.

Read Exodus 19 v 1-6 and 20 v 1-7

What is the immediate background to the Ten Commandments?

What is the focus of the first three commandments?

He Is Our God

First of all, God simply offers himself to us. For God is the abundant fullness that satisfies all; he is the everlasting well of all good things that never runs dry.

We are taught here to acknowledge one God, and no more—to stick to one, and not to suffer our hearts fantastically to dream of many. *I am your Lord, I am your God.* He is a Lord because all things are subject to him; all things bend to and obey him. He, as Lord alone, governs and upholds all things.

For God is not good to himself alone, but to us also. He desires to pour and bestow himself wholly, with all his goodness and gifts of grace, upon faithful and sincere believers.

What God Requires of Us

Second, we gather from this what the good and gracious Lord requires from us, and what our duty is and ought to be towards him. For if he will be mine, then I must be his.

Let us therefore stick to him alone. Let us obey him in all things. Let us put our trust in him, and let us call on him alone. Let us thank him for all the benefits we receive. Let us reverence him and honour him—in fear sincerely, in love most ardently, and in hope as constantly as we can.

No Other Gods

The "other god", therefore, is whatever we make for ourselves to be our god instead of the true, living and eternal God—whatever we trust, hope in, call on, love and fear; whatever we fasten our minds on, depend on, or make our treasure, help and safeguard in prosperity and adversity.

The very saints triumphant now in heaven with Christ have become like other gods to some—to those who judge very fondly of them and bestow on them the honour due to God, in worshipping and calling upon them.

Likewise, if we honour and love money or people, with the honour or love due to God, then this money and these people become like gods to us.

⊙ Apply

Do you think of God as your God, or just as the God?

Are there rival gods in your heart and affections, which need to be abandoned?

⊙ Pray

Praise the one true, living God, that he has chosen to be *our* God.

Ask God to help you root out other gods from your mind and help you trust in him alone.

~ Notes and Prayers ~

---— (Day **60**) —---

No Idolatry

Exodus 20 v 4-6 and Romans 1 v 18-25

with Heinrich Bullinger

We are forbidden to run in pilgrimage to idols, even if they are images of God himself, because this mingles superstitions with true religion.

Read Exodus 20 v 4-6 and Romans 1 v 18-25

What two exchanges are made by people under God's judgment (Romans 1 v 23, 25)?

What kinds of images of God do these people worship?

Do Not Make Any Images of Me

In the first commandment, the Lord spoke about inward worship. Now here in the second, he amends that which might be amiss in outward rituals and ceremonies. For there are many who think that God ought to be portrayed in some likeness, and to be worshipped with some bodily or visible reverence. So the purpose of this commandment is to draw them away from those gross imaginations. "I will not have you worship me according to your own inventions."

God flatly forbids the making of a graven image or other kind of idol. That is, he utterly forbids the setting up or hallowing to him of any image—of whatever shape or substance. For God is a spirit, unmeasurable, incomprehensible, present everywhere, eternal, living, giving life to and preserving all things, of a glorious majesty exalted above the heavens. Who can portray a spirit like that in any image or substance? Images are tokens of absent friends, but God is present always and everywhere.

Images Are Lies

This is why Augustine pronounced it to be horrible sacrilege for anyone to place in the church the image of God the Father sitting on a throne. Because it is detestable for anyone so much as to conceive such a likeness in his mind.

And that is also the reason why in the church before Christ we do not read that any images were erected to any saints, though there were a great number of patriarchs, judges, kings, priests, prophets, and whole troops of martyrs. The church of Christ's apostles also had no images (either of Christ himself or of other saints) set up in their places of public prayer, nor in their churches.

Whoever imagines God to be any other than indeed he is worships graven images contrary to this precept. I do not see how we can ascribe to such things the office of teaching, admonishing, and exhorting either, which are the offices and benefits of God's Holy Spirit and word. Images are merely lies. So how can something which is a lie possibly teach the truth?

⊙ Apply

Do you sometimes think of God as an old man with a white beard sitting on a throne?

Why are people tempted to these kinds of idolatry, even today?

⊙ Pray

Pray that God would forgive you if you have ever conceived of him wrongly.

Ask God to help you know him better, in the way he has revealed himself to be in Scripture.

~ Notes and Prayers ~

_____

_____

_____

_____

_____

_____

_____

_____

_____

_____

_____

_____

_____

_____

_____

_____

_____

_____

_____

_____

_____

_____

Taking the Lord's Name in Vain

Exodus 20 v 7

with Heinrich Bullinger

The Lord does not forbid us to use his name, but he charges us not to use it lightly or in vain to the detriment of his glory and honour.

Read Exodus 20 v 7

How serious is the commandment not to abuse the name of the Lord?

How might people misuse his name?

Reverence for God's Name

In this third commandment, the Lord very exquisitely, although very briefly, declares how he would be worshipped—that is, in holy reverencing of his holy name. The charge of this commandment is not to abuse the name of God, and not to use it in light and trifling matters, but to speak, to think and judge honourably, reverently and purely of God and godly things.

We unhallow the name of the Lord our God when we do not give to him all honour and glory. So let us not take the name of the Lord our God into our mouths unless it is in a matter of weight. Let us not blaspheme, curse or lie in the name of the Lord.

Shame and God's Name

Now, there are sundry ways in which we abuse the name of God. First of all, we abuse it as often as our hearts are without all reverence to God himself—when we do irreverently, filthily, wickedly and blasphemously speak of God, of his judgments, of his word and of his laws. When we with scoffing allusions apply God's words to light matters and trifles, by that means turning and drawing the Scriptures into a profane and dishonest meaning, we abuse the name of God.

Furthermore, if we deny the Lord or blush at and are ashamed of his holy gospel, because of this wicked world and the sinful people in it, then we take the Lord's name in vain, to his dishonour.

So let us not be ashamed of God our Father, of his truth and true religion. Let us not be ashamed of Christ our redeemer, nor of his cross. But let us be ashamed of errors, idolatries, of the world and vanity, of lies and sin. Let us reverently and devoutly both speak and think of God, his works and his word. Let the law of God be holy to us, let his gospel be revered in our eyes, and let the doctrine of the patriarchs, prophets and apostles be esteemed by us as that which came from God himself.

⊙ Apply

How would you respond to someone who was rude about the apostle Paul's doctrine, but claimed to hold Jesus' words in high esteem?

What could you say next time you hear someone misuse the name of the Lord, which would give him the honour he deserves?

⊘ Pray

Ask for forgiveness for the times when you have thought too lightly of God and his name.

Ask God to help you speak and think of him more reverently, and not be ashamed of his words.

~ Notes and Prayers ~

Day
62

Remember
the Sabbath

Exodus 20 v 8-11 and Deuteronomy 5 v 12-15

with Heinrich Bullinger

The command to remember the Sabbath day and keep it holy belongs both to the inward and outward service of God.

Read Exodus 20 v 8-11 and Deuteronomy 5 v 12-15

What positive things was an Israelite to do on the Sabbath day?

What was the motivation for remembering the Sabbath day?

The Spiritual Sabbath

Sabbath means rest and ceasing from work. And this here I think worthy to be noted, that the Lord said not simply, "Sanctify the Sabbath", but, "Remember the Sabbath day, to keep it holy" (Exodus 20 v 8, KJV)—meaning by this that the Sabbath was ordained of old and given first of all to the ancient fathers, and then again renewed by the Lord and beaten into the memory of the people of Israel.

The Sabbath itself has sundry meanings. For first of all, Scripture makes mention of a certain spiritual and continual Sabbath. In this Sabbath we rest from work, in abstaining from sin, and doing our best not to work our own works, but in ceasing from these to suffer God to work in us, and wholly to submit our bodies to the government of his good Spirit.

After this Sabbath follows that eternal Sabbath and everlasting rest, of which Isaiah 58 and Isaiah 66 speak, and also Hebrews 4. But God is truly worshipped when we, ceasing from evil and obeying God's Holy Spirit, exercise ourselves in the study of good works. So let us (my brethren) in these our mortal bodies, endeavour with an unwearied good and holy will to sanctify the Sabbath that pleases the Lord so well.

Rest and Recreation

Faith and religion bid you to give rest to your servants and family. Indeed, they command you to egg them on and compel them, if they are slow to take up the holy and profitable work of the Lord. Moreover, the Lord's mind is that they which labour should also refresh and recreate themselves, for things which lack a resting time can never long endure.

Yet nevertheless those who are Christians should not forget the words of Christ in the Gospel, where he says, "The Sabbath was made for man, not man for the Sabbath. So the Son of Man is Lord even of the Sabbath" (Mark 2 v 27-28). Our Saviour gave us an example to follow, when on the Sabbath day he did works of charity and mercy.

⊙ Apply

Do you keep the Sabbath by ceasing from evil and obeying God's Holy Spirit?

Do you keep the principle of weekly rest, and allow others to do so?

⊙ Pray

Thank God for the eternal Sabbath and everlasting rest in store for us in the new creation.

Ask God to help you see how to please him more and more with regard to this commandment.

~ Notes and Prayers ~

_____
_____
_____
_____
_____
_____
_____
_____
_____
_____
_____
_____
_____
_____
_____
_____
_____
_____
_____
_____
_____
_____
_____
_____

Day

63

Christst
for Us

Romans 8 v 1-4

with Thomas Cranmer

All the good works that we can do are unable to earn our salvation, which comes freely by the mere mercy of God because of Christ's work on our behalf.

Read Romans 8 v 1-4

What do we contribute to our salvation?

How can you be saved if you haven't fulfilled the law?

Faith and Works

Three things must concur and go together in our justification. First, on God's part, his great mercy and grace. Second, on Christ's part, justice—that is, the satisfaction of God's justice, or the price of our redemption by the offering of his body and shedding of his blood, with fulfilling of the law, perfectly and thoroughly. And third, on our part, true and lively faith in the merits of Jesus Christ, which yet is not ours, but by God's working in us.

Paul declares here nothing upon our behalf concerning our justification, but only a true and lively faith, which nevertheless is the gift of God. And yet that faith does not exclude repentance, hope, love, dread and the fear of God; these things are joined with faith in everyone who is justified. But although they are all present together in the one who is justified, yet they do not all justify together.

Nor does faith exclude the justice of our good works, necessarily to be done afterwards of duty towards God. For we are clearly bound to serve God in doing good deeds commanded by him in his holy Scripture, all the days of our life. But works *are* excluded from faith, in the sense that we may not do them in order to be made good by doing them.

The Precious Jewels

Our justification comes freely, by the mere mercy of God. We need such great and free mercy because no one in the whole world is able of themselves to pay any part towards their ransom. And yet it pleased our heavenly Father, of his infinite mercy, without any desert or deserving in us, to prepare for us the most precious jewels of Christ's body and blood. By these our ransom is fully paid, the law fulfilled, and his justice fully satisfied.

Christ is now the righteousness of all those who truly believe in him. He *for them* paid their ransom by his death. He *for them* fulfilled the law in his life. So that now, in him and by him, every true Christian may be called a fulfiller of the law.

⊙ Apply

Can you say in a sentence what part our good works have alongside faith?

Meditate on the fact that Jesus not only paid your ransom but also fulfilled the law in your place.

⊙ Pray

Praise God that he not only saves us by faith alone apart from works (Romans 3 v 28), but that even faith is a gift from him.

Thank Jesus for all he has done in your place: paying your ransom, fulfilling the law, and satisfying God's justice.

~ Notes and Prayers ~

Honour
Your Parents

Exodus 20 v 12 and Ephesians 6 v 1-9

with Heinrich Bullinger

H aving been taught how to love God, now in the second table or section of the Ten Commandments we hear how to love our neighbours.

Read Exodus 20 v 12 and Ephesians 6 v 1-9

What is the link between obeying certain other people and obeying God (Ephesians 6 v 1-9)?

What promises are associated with such obedience?

Deserving Our Respect

As the first table of the Ten Commandments taught us to love God, so the second teaches us the charity that is due to our neighbour. It instructs us what we owe to our neighbour and how we may live in this world honestly, civilly and in quiet peace among ourselves. For our good God would have us to live well and quietly.

Rightly does the Lord begin the second table with honouring of our parents (Deuteronomy 5 v 16). Greater are the good turns that parents do for their children, greater is the cost and labour that they bestow on them, greater is the care, grief and trouble which they take for them, than anyone (however eloquent) is able to express.

We also include here the country in which someone was born, which fed, fostered, adorned and defended them. And we also include rulers and magistrates in the name and title of "parents", for senators and princes are in the holy Scriptures called the fathers and pastors of the people (e.g. 2 Kings 5 v 13; Isaiah 22 v 21). Obedience to earthly masters, and to the ministers, doctors and pastors of the church, is also contained within this commandment.

Honour

To honour, here, means to magnify, to esteem well, and to do reverence as to a thing ordained by God. It means to acknowledge, to love and to give praise for a benefit received at God's hand—as for a thing given from heaven that is holy, profitable and necessary. To honour is to be dutiful and to obey, and so to obey as if it were to God himself, by whom we know that our obedience is commanded, and to whom we are sure that our service is acceptable.

You honour your parents when you do not contemptuously despise them or ungratefully neglect them. However, we must not obey either our parents or magistrates if they themselves shall do or else command us to do things that are wicked and unjust. For the later commandments still have reference to those that went before, which tell us to love God above all.

⊘ Apply

Do you honour your parents, and others who may have God-given authority over you?

How can we show that we honour our country and the authorities in it, at the same time as distancing ourselves from any wickedness and injustice in it?

⊙ Pray

Thank God for giving you parents, and for all they did/do for you.

Ask God for wisdom to work out what honouring them and others means at your stage of life, and for strength to do it.

~ Notes and Prayers ~

Do Not Murder

Exodus 20 v 13 and Matthew 5 v 21-26

with Heinrich Bullinger

Here are many steps to the evil sin of murder—destroying people made in God's image—especially envy and anger, which we must root out of our hearts.

Read Exodus 20 v 13 and Matthew 5 v 21-26

Why does Jesus include anger in his exposition of the sixth commandment?

Why is the penalty for this sin so strong?

Angry Words

In this precept, "Do not murder", justice and innocence are commanded and commended to us. It is also provided that no one should hurt another's life or body, and so in this law a charge is given to everyone to maintain peace and quietness.

For the Lord does not simply forbid murder, but all other things bound up with murder. Provoking others to anger is utterly forbidden. Slanderous taunts and brawling speeches are flatly prohibited. Strife, wrath and envy are plainly commanded to be suppressed. We can see this in the way Christ our Lord himself interpreted this law in Matthew 5. Anger, slander, brawling, and all other tokens of a mind moved to utter ill words, are flatly forbidden.

It is because so few of us obey this sound and wholesome doctrine of the Lord's that so many great and troublesome tumults happen among us. For small is the wealth and power of those that obey the word of God, but great is the rest and quietness of their consciences. And what pleasure, I ask you, do infinite riches bring to people, since with them a person cannot likely be without troublesome cares of mind, great turmoils and lack of a quiet life. This law therefore, which tends to no other end but to teach us the way to lead a sweet and pleasant life, wholly takes from our mind such immoderate affections as anger and envy—two of the most pestilent evils that reign among mankind.

Envy

We must not allow our adversary the devil to fasten his foot in our hearts. Through anger, he creeps into our minds, little by little, and by continual wrath he works out envy, by which he captivates and perverts the whole person, with all their senses, words and works. For envy is anger grown into custom by long continuance, which does for the most part vex, burn and mangle the one who envies more then the one who is envied. It is an endless evil—and counterfeit Christians, addicted to envy, should be ashamed of it and learn to blush.

⊙ Apply

Have anger or envy got their claws into your heart anywhere?

How can you prevent anger or annoyance becoming something worse?

⊙ Pray

Ask God to forgive you for any anger, malice or envy in your heart and words.

Ask God to enable you to sort out any relationship difficulties you may have before they get to this point.

~ Notes and Prayers ~

_____

_____

_____

_____

_____

_____

_____

_____

_____

_____

_____

_____

_____

_____

_____

_____

_____

_____

_____

_____

_____

Do Not
Commit Adultery

Exodus 20 v 14 and 1 Thessalonians 4 v 1-8

with Heinrich Bullinger

G od gives a commandment to protect honourable marriage, for the true
sanctifying of the body against adultery and wandering lusts.

Read Exodus 20 v 14 and 1 Thessalonians 4 v 1-8

*How are Christians to be different to others in their sexual ethics (1 Thessalonians 4
v 3-6)?*

Why does Paul stress the divine origin of these instructions (e.g. verses 2 and 8)?

God Ordained Marriage

Wedlock or matrimony is an alliance or holy joining together of man and woman,
coupled and brought into one by mutual consent of them both. Its purpose is that
they, using all things in common between them, may live in purity and train up
their children in the fear of the Lord.

God appointed other good and necessary rules for mankind's good by the means
and ministry of angels and chosen people. But he himself did immediately, without
the ministry of any person, ordain matrimony. He himself established and ratified
it with laws for the purpose. He himself did couple the first married folks and
he, being the true High Priest, did himself bless the couple whom he did so join
together. By this we may easily gather the excellent dignity of marriage. For God

ordained it—and he ordained it in Paradise, when mankind was, as yet, free from all kinds of calamities.

Sexual Holiness

Married couples are to be mindful of the faith which they give and take, that they do not falsely deceive one another, but keep the promise that they make, and keep it sincerely both in body and mind. Let neither of them lust after the body of a stranger, nor conceive a hatred or loathing of their wedded spouse.

The Lord in his law has expressly named adultery alone, but along with that it is also understood to include all kinds of lust and luxury, and all other things which encourage and stir up fire in people to sexual immodesty, which he forbids as severely as adultery itself. The Lord in the Gospel (Matthew 5 v 27-30) not only forbids the outward work of adultery, but the very affection also and wanton lust of the heart and mind.

So then, in this precept every unclean thought, all ribald talk and filthiness of bodily deeds are utterly forbidden, as is anything which incites or allures us to unlawful lusts. This seventh commandment forbids all intemperance, and instead commands holiness, and the clean and lawful use of all the members of the whole body.

⊙ Apply

Do you tend to sail close to the winds of sexual temptation and immodesty, or try to aim at self-control and holiness?

How can you encourage others in this area by what you watch, what you read, what you wear or what you talk about?

⊙ Pray

Confess your failure to perfectly love God with all your heart, soul, mind and strength in this part of life.

Ask God, "who gives you his Holy Spirit" (1 Thessalonians 4 v 8), to help you please him in body and mind.

~ Notes and Prayers ~

Do Not
Steal

Exodus 20 v 15 and Romans 13 v 6-10

with Heinrich Bullinger

I n his law, which he ordains for our health, convenience and peace, God prescribes how we are to obtain and use earthly goods.

Read Exodus 20 v 15 and Romans 13 v 6-10

What sorts of debts are mentioned in Romans 13 v 6-10?

What positive reasons are given for not stealing?

Justice and Riches

For the sustaining and nourishing of our lives and families we have need of earthly riches. Next, therefore, after the commandments touching the preservation of life and the holy keeping of wedlock's knot, in this eighth commandment a law is given for the true getting, possessing, using, and bestowing of wealth and worldly substance. The purpose of this is that we should not get these things by theft or evil means, that we should not possess them unjustly, or use and spend them unlawfully.

Justice requires us to use riches well, and to give to everyone what is rightfully theirs. So the law of God says, "You shall not steal". These words again are few in number, but they are abundant in meaning. For in this precept theft itself is utterly forbidden, all shifting subtleties are flatly prohibited, deceit and guile are banished, all deceptive trickery is clean cut off. Covetousness, idleness, prodigality, or lavish spending, and all unjust dealing is excluded. Moreover, charge is here given for the maintenance of justice, especially in contracts and bargains.

Generous Ownership

Wonderful turmoils are raised up and begun among the people of this world about the getting, possessing and spending of earthly riches. The proper owning and possessing of goods is not by this precept prohibited, but we are forbidden to get them unjustly, to possess them unlawfully, and to spend them wickedly. Indeed, by this commandment, the proper ownership of things is lawfully ordained and firmly established. For what can you steal if all things are common to all?

But let everyone pick out and choose an honest and profitable occupation, and fly from idleness, as a plague or contagious disease. As Paul says, "The one who is unwilling to work shall not eat" (see 2 Thessalonians 3 v 6-15). For God does not assist the slothful. Rather, "anyone who has been stealing must steal no longer, but must work, doing something useful with their own hands, that they may have something to share with those in need" (Ephesians 4 v 28).

⊘ Apply

Are you busy at work (whether in paid employment or otherwise), or just a busybody (2 Thessalonians 3 v 11)?

Is there a debt of some kind that you need to pay to someone?

⊙ Pray

Thank God for all the possessions he has allowed you to have and use for his glory.

Ask him to show you how you can better use these good gifts for the good of others too.

~ Notes and Prayers ~

Day
68

Do Not Lie

Exodus 20 v 16 and James 3 v 1-10

with Heinrich Bullinger

The ninth commandment concerns bearing false witness, because God cares about truth, not only in a court of law but also in all our speaking.

Read Exodus 20 v 16 and James 3 v 1-10

Why is the tongue so dangerous (James 3 v 3-8)?

Why is it so difficult to control?

True Testimony

This law commands us to use our tongues well, that we neither privately nor publicly harm our neighbour, either in their life, good name or riches, by word or writing or otherwise. All things are forbidden that are against truth and sincerity. There is required from us all simplicity, plain speaking and telling of the truth. Briefly, we are all commanded to endeavour mutually to maintain plain dealing and truth.

First of all in this commandment it is forbidden for everyone in the court before a judge to bear false witness. It is lawful to be a true witness, especially if a magistrate demands it of you. But in giving testimony, those who speak must have regard for God alone, and simple truth. They must lay aside all evil affections, hatred, fear and all taking of sides, and must hide nothing. They must not devise anything of their own imagination, nor corrupt the meaning of someone's words.

Slander and Backbiting

We may gather by many arguments that it is a heinous crime falsely to slander and wickedly to backbite our brethren and neighbours. For there is scarcely anything that disgraces us as much as backbiting does. We are made in the image and likeness of God, that we may be the children of God; but false accusations make children of God into children of the devil. We all abhor and utterly detest the name of the devil, but if you are a wrongful slanderer, then you are the very same as that which you do so detest. For the devil takes his name from wrongful accusing, and is called a slanderer *(the Greek word for the devil, diabolos, means "slanderer").*

God hates backbiting and slander. In Proverbs 22 v 1 Solomon testifies that "a good name is more desirable than great riches". A good reputation is a precious treasure. When, therefore, the fame and good name of a person is threatened by the false reports and slanders of a wicked tongue, the chief jewel that a person has is put in jeopardy.

⊙ Apply

Is it true that "sticks and stones may break my bones but words can never hurt me"?

When do you find it most difficult to tell the absolute truth, and why?

⊙ Pray

Praise the Lord Jesus, who never once told a lie or said anything untrue or misused the power of speech.

Ask God to help you control your tongue better, to please him and protect others.

~ Notes and Prayers ~

_____
_____
_____
_____
_____
_____
_____
_____
_____
_____
_____
_____
_____
_____
_____
_____
_____
_____
_____

Day
69

Do Not Covet

Exodus 20 v 17 and James 4 v 1-10

with Heinrich Bullinger

G od, in his law, requires not only outward holiness but inward purity of the mind, the soul and all our affections.

Read Exodus 20 v 17 and James 4 v 1-10

Why do people fight (James 4 v 1-3)?

What should they do instead?

Good Desires

In this law, coveting is especially forbidden—evil longing and corrupt desiring. We must here be able with discretion to judge between that good affection, which God first created in mankind, and that other motion, the root of evil that grows in our nature by the descent of corruption from our first father, Adam.

There was in Adam, before his fall, a certain good appetite with pleasure and delight. And this good appetite or desire came from God himself, who made both Adam and all his affections good at the first. And even today, there are in us certain natural affections and desires which of themselves are not to be counted as sins, unless by corruption of original vice they pass the bounds for which they are ordained.

Evil Desires

But in the tenth commandment, desire is used in the worse sense, and is taken for the coveting of evil things. This is the fruit of our corrupt nature, of original sin, whose seat is in our heart and is the fountain and headspring of all sin and wickedness that is to be found in us mortals. It is a motion or affection of the mind which lusts against God and his law, and stirs us up to wickedness, although the consent or deed itself does not immediately follow. But if the deed does follow the lust, then the sin increases by steps and degrees.

This evil and unlawful affection comes from our natural corruption and lies hidden in our nature. It betrays its presence in our hearts by rebelling against the purity of God's law and majesty, and is the very sin which is in this commandment condemned. For although there are some who think that such motions, diseases, blemishes and affections of the mind are not sins, yet God, by forbidding them in this law, flatly condemns them.

Those whose hearts are wrapped in lusts, diseased and spotted with the poison of original guilt, shall not see God. So this law convicts us all of sin, and of damnation. It drives us to Christ to be saved.

⊙ Apply

Do you realise that your evil thoughts and inclinations are themselves sinful, not just when you put them into practice?

What is the difference between the sinful desires you've thought about or felt recently, and temptation?

⊙ Pray

Thank God that because Jesus has taken the punishment we deserve for our sins—both our original corruption of nature and our actual transgressions—we are saved.

Ask God to give you integrity of heart and life, to both desire truly and live rightly for his glory.

~ Notes and Prayers ~

Day
7O

For the Glory of Christ

Revelation 1 v 4-8

with Thomas Cranmer

J ustification by faith alone has always been the strong rock and foundation of Christian religion because it gives all glory to God.

Read Revelation 1 v 4-8

Why does John ascribe glory to Jesus in verses 5-6?

What will be the reaction of those who opposed Jesus, in verse 7?

Not a Novel Doctrine

Consider diligently these words: *without works, by faith only, freely, we receive remission of our sins.* What can be spoken more plainly than to say that freely, without works, by faith only, we obtain remission of our sins?

That we are justified by faith only, freely and without works, we do often read in the best and most ancient writers. Hilary of Poitiers says these words plainly: "Faith alone justifies". And Basil of Caesarea, a Greek author, writes that "this is a perfect and a whole rejoicing in God, when a person acknowledges that they lack true justice and righteousness, and are justified only by faith in Christ".

Beside Hilary, Basil, and Ambrose, we read the same in Origen, Chrysostom, Cyprian, Augustine, Prosper, Oecomenius, Photius, Bernardus, Anselm, and many other authors, Greek and Latin.

But this proposition—that we are justified by faith only, freely and without works—is spoken in order clearly to take away all merit of our works, as being insufficient to deserve our justification at God's hands. Thereby it most plainly expresses our weakness and the goodness of God, the great infirmity of ourselves and the might and power of God, the imperfection of our own works and the most abundant grace of our Saviour, Christ. And thereby wholly to ascribe the merit and deserving of our justification to Christ only and his most precious blood-shedding.

A Doctrine That Brings Glory to God

This faith the holy Scripture teaches. This is the strong rock and foundation of Christian religion. This doctrine all old and ancient authors of Christ's church do approve.

This doctrine advances and sets forth the true glory of Christ, and suppresses the vainglory of mankind. Whoever denies this is not to be thought of as a true Christian, nor for a setter forth of Christ's glory, but for an adversary of Christ and his gospel, and for a setter forth of mankind's vainglory.

⊙ Apply

Meditate on the idea that true, orthodox doctrine brings glory to Christ, whereas false doctrine exalts mankind at God's expense. Can you think of other examples of this?

The Reformers claimed to be rediscovering true doctrine rather than making it up afresh. How important do you think that is?

⊙ Pray

Praise God that all the glory for our salvation goes to him alone and not to us.

Ask God to help you give him all the glory in your life and in your doctrine.

~ Notes and Prayers ~

Day
71

A Life
of Blessing

Psalm 1

with John Calvin

Today we begin our final series of studies, looking at the Psalms with the aid of John Calvin. He begins by saying, "Instead of allowing ourselves to be deceived by the imaginary happiness of the ungodly, let us keep God's word and providence ever before our eyes".

Read Psalm 1

What does the blessed person delight in, which the ungodly do not?

What do the various contrasts between the two kinds of people mean?

Delight in the Word

Whoever collected the Psalms into one volume appears to have placed this psalm at the beginning, by way of preface. It impresses on all the godly the duty of meditating on the law of God. The sum and substance of the whole is that those who apply their hearts to the pursuit of heavenly wisdom are blessed; whereas the unbelieving despisers of God, although for a time they may reckon themselves happy, shall at length have a most miserable end.

It shall always be well with God's devout servants, whose constant endeavour it is to make progress in the study of his law. The greater part of mankind are accustomed to deride the conduct of the saints as mere childish simplicity, and to regard their labour as entirely thrown away. So it is important that the righteous should be confirmed in the way of holiness, by the consideration of the miserable condition of all those without the blessing of God.

God is favourable to none but those who zealously devote themselves to the study of divine truth. So before asserting the blessedness of such students of the divine law, the psalm-writer warns them to beware of being carried away by the ungodliness of the multitude around them.

Hate Ungodliness

All people naturally desire and seek after happiness, and those who have departed farthest from righteousness in the gratification of their lusts are often accounted happy, because they obtain the desires of their heart. This psalm, on the contrary, teaches that the ungodly are miserable, and that those who do not withdraw from their company shall be involved in the same destruction with them.

Servants of God must endeavour utterly to hate the life of the ungodly. The psalm-writer does not keep his eye on the prosperous condition they boast about for a short time, but his mind is seriously pondering the destruction which awaits them. Although the ungodly now live prosperously, yet by and by they shall be like chaff. By this form of speech, the Holy Spirit teaches us to contemplate things with the eye of faith.

⊘ Apply

What would you say to someone who said that unbelievers are the strong and happy ones whereas Christians just seem to be wasting their time and effort?

How can you delight in and meditate on God's word more?

⊘ Pray

Thank God for his word, the Bible, and for graciously revealing himself and his ways to us in the pages of this amazing book.

Ask God to help you see things in this world with the eyes of faith, from the perspective of eternity.

~ Notes and Prayers ~

_____

_____

_____

_____

_____

_____

_____

_____

_____

_____

_____

_____

_____

_____

_____

_____

_____

_____

_____

_____

_____

_____

_____

_____

Day
72

Christ and His Enemies

Psalm 2

with John Calvin

It is not at all unusual if the world begins to rage as soon as a throne is erected—for Christ and his kingdom rises from obscurity into open view.

Read Psalm 2

Why is the rebellious plot in the psalm bound to fail?

What does God do as he confidently laughs this off?

David's Kingdom

David (the author of this psalm, see Acts 4 v 25-26) boasts that his kingdom would be perpetual, though attacked by a vast multitude of powerful enemies, because it was upheld by the power of God. In spite of his enemies, it would be extended even to the uttermost ends of the earth. Therefore, he exhorts kings and other rulers to lay aside their pride, and receive with submissive minds the yoke laid upon them by God, as it would be vain for them to attempt to shake it off. All this contains a prophecy concerning the future kingdom of Christ.

David confesses that he had a difficult battle to fight, because whole nations with their kings had conspired against him. But he courageously boasts that their attempts were vain, because they waged war, not against mortal man, but against God himself. Those who endeavoured to overthrow him might be strengthened by powerful armies, yet their tumults and counsels would prove vain and ineffective.

Christ's Kingdom

That David prophesied concerning Christ is clearly manifest from this, that he knew his own kingdom to be merely a shadow. And in order to learn to apply to Christ whatever David, in times past, sang concerning himself, we must hold this principle—he was made king, not so much for his own sake as to be a "type" of the Redeemer. David's earthly kingdom was a kind of downpayment to God's ancient people of the eternal kingdom, which at length was truly established in the person of Christ. So those things which David declares concerning himself are not violently, or even allegorically, applied to Christ, but were truly predicted concerning him.

That the kingdom of Christ is here described by the Spirit of prophecy is sufficiently confirmed for us by the apostles who, seeing the ungodly conspiring against Christ, arm themselves in prayer with this doctrine (Acts 4 v 24-28). Let this, therefore, be held as a settled point, that all who do not submit themselves to the authority of Christ make war against God. They furiously assault heaven itself, but we may safely laugh them to scorn.

⊘ Apply

In what ways do the nations or rulers and governments oppose the kingdom of Christ today?

Have you "kissed [the] son" (Psalm 2 v 12)? Do you serve Jesus loyally and gladly?

⊘ Pray

Praise Jesus that he is a strong and mighty king who has defeated all our enemies and whose kingdom shall have no end.

Ask him to help you "rejoice with trembling" as you submit to his rule over your own life.

~ Notes and Prayers ~

Day

73

Salvation
Belongs to the Lord

Psalm 3

with John Calvin

The power of God is infinite and invincible against all the assaults, outrages, conspiracies and forces of the whole world.

Read Psalm 3

What difficulty is David facing here?

What is he confident that God will do to help him?

God Won't Save Them!

David has been driven from his kingdom (2 Samuel 15 v 13-14) and pressed down with utter despair of relief from every earthly quarter. This disaster was brought upon him by God for his own fault (2 Samuel 16 v 8), but he does not cease to call upon God. He supports himself with God's promise against the greatest terrors, against the mockery and cruel assaults of his enemies and, finally, against death itself.

After he had humbled himself before God, he took courage. Being well assured of having obtained forgiveness, he was fully persuaded that God was on his side, and knew that he would always preside over his kingdom. Nevertheless, he complained about the whole faction involved in the conspiracy, because he knew that they wickedly rose up for the purpose of frustrating the decree of God.

Although the whole world with one voice should attempt to drive us to despair, instead of listening to it we ought rather to give ear to God alone, and always cherish within us the hope of the salvation which he has promised. But if our enemies, in persecuting us, rather fight against God than against us, then let us be confident of our safety under the protection of him whose grace they despise and trample underfoot.

God Has Saved Us!

This is how the servants of God should act when molested by the wicked. Having mourned over their own sins, and humbly thrown themselves on the mercy of God, they ought to entertain no doubt of the help of God when undeservedly subjected to evil treatment. God will help, especially when, by their being evilly treated, the truth of God is opposed. They ought to be greatly encouraged, and glory in the assurance that God without doubt will maintain the truth of his own promises against such treacherous characters.

David acknowledges the dispersion of this wicked conspiracy is due to the care which God had about the safety of his people, the church. The church shall always be delivered from the calamities which befall her, because God will never withdraw his grace and blessing from her.

⊙ Apply

Do you think it is possible for God to still be "on our side" even if we have sinned against him?

In what ways can we be confident of God's help when people fight against God and his truth today?

⊙ Pray

Praise God that he is the one who brings us salvation, and that his promises have the power to protect us and lift our heads in the midst of despair.

Ask the Lord to continue to protect his truth and his church today where you see it is most in danger from foes.

~ Notes and Prayers ~

Day
74

How Majestic
Is Your Name

Psalm 8

with John Calvin

As he reflects on God's fatherly goodness towards mankind, David is not content with simply giving thanks for it, but is enraptured by the contemplation of it.

Read Psalm 8

What has God done?

What is the role of human beings?

How Amazing!

David sets before his eyes the wonderful power and glory of God in the creation and government of the universe. He insists principally on the theme of God's infinite goodness towards us. There is presented to us in the whole order of nature the most abundant matter for showing forth the glory of God. But since we are more powerfully affected with what we ourselves experience, David here expressly celebrates the special favour which God manifests towards mankind. For this, of all the subjects which come under our contemplation, is the brightest mirror in which we can behold God's glory.

The Holy Spirit intended by this to awaken us from our lethargy and indifference, so that we may not content ourselves with celebrating the infinite love of God and the innumerable benefits which we receive at his hand, in a sparing and frosty manner—but may, rather, apply our whole hearts to this holy exercise, and our highest efforts into it.

How Gracious!

We must be careful to note the design of David, which is to enhance, by this comparison, the infinite goodness of God. For it is a wonderful thing that the Creator of heaven, whose glory is so surpassingly great as to ravish us with the highest admiration, condescends so far as graciously to take upon him the care of the human race. Whoever, therefore, is not astonished and deeply affected at this miracle, is more than ungrateful and stupid.

In creation, God gave a demonstration of his infinite grace and fatherly love towards us, which ought to strike us with amazement. David here confines his attention to God's earthly benefits, but it is our duty to rise higher, and to contemplate the invaluable treasures of the kingdom of heaven which he has unfolded in Christ, and all the gifts which belong to the spiritual life. By reflecting upon these, our hearts are inflamed with love for God, we are stirred up to the practice of godliness, and we cannot allow ourselves to become slothful and remiss in celebrating his praises.

⊙ Apply

Today, "consider [the] heavens" and "the work of [God's] fingers" (v 3), and how majestic the Creator of it all must be.

Do you ever behold his glory in "the brightest mirror" by contemplating the special favour God has shown to humanity, and to you in particular?

⊙ Pray

Praise God for his majesty and power in creating and sustaining the universe.

Ask God to help you grasp how spectacular his grace towards you really is.

~ Notes and Prayers ~

Day
75

True
Happiness

Psalm 16

with John Calvin

Full and substantial happiness and protection consists in resting in God alone, who never allows his own people to lack any good thing.

Read Psalm 16

What is David devoting himself to?

What is David looking forward to?

Preserve Me

In the beginning, David commends himself to the protection of God. He then meditates upon the benefits which he received from God, and so stirs himself up to thanksgiving. He surrenders and devotes himself entirely to God, affirming that he will have nothing to do with superstitions. God is ready to assist all of us, provided we rely upon him with a sure and steadfast faith. He takes under his protection none but those who commit themselves to him with their whole heart.

The Excellent Ones

The only way of serving God aright is to endeavour to do good to his holy servants. When people mutually exert themselves in doing good to one another, this is to yield to God right and acceptable service. David also intimates that he will unite himself with the devout worshippers of God, and be their associate or companion—even as all the children of God ought to be joined together by the bond of brotherly unity, that they may all serve and call upon their common Father with the same affection and zeal. There is no sacrifice more acceptable to God than when we sincerely and heartily connect ourselves with the society of the righteous, and being knit together by the sacred bond of godliness, cultivate and maintain with them brotherly goodwill.

Fullness of Joy

When God is reconciled to us, we have all things which are necessary for perfect happiness. Fullness of joy is contrasted with the vanishing allurements and pleasures of this transitory world, which divert their miserable followers for a time but in the end leave them unsatisfied, famished and disappointed. They may intoxicate and glut themselves with pleasures to the greatest excess but instead of being satisfied, they rather become wearied of them through loathing. The pleasures of this world vanish away like dreams. David, therefore, testifies that true and solid joy in which our minds may rest will never be found anywhere else but in God. Therefore none but the faithful, who are contented with his grace alone, can be truly and perfectly happy.

⊙ Apply

Are you as devoted to "the noble ones", the church, as David says he delights to be?

In Acts 2 v 24-33 and Acts 13 v 35, the apostles say this psalm is talking about Jesus. Why do you think it was particularly appropriate for him?

⊘ Pray

Praise the Lord that he protects and blesses his people as we trust in him for fullness of joy.

Ask God to help you look to him, his people and the counsel of his word for your true happiness, rather than looking to things which leave the ungodly unsatisfied and sorrowful in the end.

~ Notes and Prayers ~

Day
76

Why Have You Forsaken Me?

Psalm 22

with John Calvin

D avid gives chief place to faith in claiming God as his God, even as he utters
his suffering complaint. His faith—and Christ's—is vindicated in the end.

Read Psalm 22

What signs are there that David still trusts God, despite his suffering and anguish?

Which parts of this psalm make you think not just of human suffering but of Christ's crucifixion?

Faithful Complaint

David complains that he is reduced to such distress that he is like a man in despair.
But after having recounted the calamities with which he was so severely afflicted,
he emerges from the abyss of temptations and, gathering courage, comforts himself with the assurance of deliverance. At the same time, he sets before us a "type"
of Christ, who he knew by the Spirit of prophecy would be humbled in marvellous
and unusual ways before his exaltation by the Father.

The people of God, in wrestling with themselves, on the one hand discover the
weakness of the flesh, and on the other give evidence of their faith. That David
sustained the assaults of temptation, without being overwhelmed, or swallowed up
by them, may be easily gathered from his words. Greatly oppressed with sorrow, he
still breaks into the language of faith and assurance: "My God! my God!"

There is not one of the godly who does not daily experience the same thing. According to the judgment of the flesh, they think they are cast off and forsaken by God. But at the same time, they apprehend by faith the grace of God, which is hidden from the eye of sense and reason. Thus it comes to pass, that contrary affections are mingled and interwoven in the prayers of the faithful.

Suffering Saviour

Our Saviour, Jesus Christ, when hanging on the cross, made use of these very words (Matthew 27 v 46). Christ was the only begotten Son of God, and yet he was so penetrated with grief, seized with such great mental turmoil, as to cry out that God his Father had forsaken him.

As Jesus became our representative, and took upon him our sins, it was certainly necessary that he should appear before the judgment seat of God as a sinner. From this proceeded the terror and dread which constrained him to pray for deliverance from death, because there was before his eyes the curse of God to which all who are sinners are exposed. Yet Christ's resurrection bears witness that his prayer was heard.

⊘ Apply

As the cry of a suffering believer, what comfort does the psalm give you in your own struggles?

As a prophecy of Christ (especially verses 1, 16, 17, 18, 27-31), how does it fuel your prayers?

⊘ Pray

Praise the Lord Jesus, who bore the punishment for our sins, in our place, on the cross.

Ask God to give you the same persevering faith in the midst of troubles as David had.

~ Notes and Prayers ~

Day

77

Devilish Faith

James 2 v 14-26

with Thomas Cranmer

Our duty is not to pass the time of this present life unfruitfully and idly, not caring how few good works we do to the glory of God and profit of our neighbours.

Read James 2 v 14-26

Is it possible for true faith (which alone justifies us) to remain idle?

What does James mean by the demons having faith / believing in God (v 19)?

Orthodox but Unsaved

That faith which brings forth (without repentance) either evil works or no good works is not a right, pure and lively faith, but a dead, devilish and counterfeit faith. Even the devils know and believe that Christ suffered a most painful death for our sakes to redeem us from eternal death, and that he rose again from death on the third day. They believe that he ascended into heaven, and that he sits on the right hand of the Father, and at the last end of this world shall come again to judge both the living and the dead.

These articles of our faith, the devils believe, and so they believe all things that are written in the New and Old Testaments to be true. And yet for all this faith, they are but devils, remaining still in their damnable state, lacking the very true Christian faith.

True Faith

For the right and true Christian faith is not only to believe that holy Scripture and all the previously mentioned articles of our faith are true, but also to have a sure trust and confidence in God's merciful promises, to be saved from everlasting damnation by Christ. From this follows a loving heart to obey his commandments.

And this true Christian faith, no devil has—nor any human who, in the outward profession of their mouth, and in the outward receiving of the sacraments, in coming to church and in all other outward appearances, seems to be a Christian, and yet in their living and deeds shows the contrary.

For how can someone have this true faith, this sure trust and confidence in God—that by the merits of Christ their sins are cancelled and they are reconciled to the favour of God and are partakers of the kingdom of heaven by Christ—when they live ungodly lives and deny Christ in their deeds? Surely, no such ungodly person can have this faith and trust in God. For as they know Christ to be the only Saviour of the world, so they know also that wicked people shall not possess the kingdom of God.

⊙ Apply

Tremble that there is more orthodox theology in hell than in many palaces, pulpits and pews, and yet it does the demonic minions of Satan no spiritual good at all.

Are you orthodox in your head but not trusting in God's promises in your heart or life? Talk to someone you trust about any struggles you might have here.

⊙ Pray

Pray that you would truly trust and rely on Christ each day, and not merely appear to say and do the right things among Christian friends.

Pray for any you know who profess with their lips but do not live a biblically-defined godly life, that they would repent and not be excluded from God's kingdom.

~ Notes and Prayers ~

Day
78

Trusting God in the Good Times

Psalm 23

with John Calvin

Those who enjoy the greatest abundance of outward good things are empty and famished if God is not their Shepherd.

Read Psalm 23

What are all the good things David is enjoying in his life at this moment?

Who is responsible for that?

Thanksgiving

This psalm contains simply a thanksgiving, from which it appears that it was composed when David had obtained peaceable possession of the kingdom, and lived in prosperity. He does not wish, in the time of his great prosperity, to be like worldly men—who, when they seem to themselves to be fortunate, bury God in forgetfulness and luxuriously plunge themselves into their pleasures. So he delights himself in God, the author of all the blessings which he enjoyed.

David acknowledges that the state of tranquillity in which he now lives, and his exemption from all inconveniences and troubles, is owing to the goodness of God. He also trusts that, through God's providence, he will continue happy even to the close of his life.

A Ladder to God

Although God, by his benefits, gently attracts us to himself by a taste of his fatherly sweetness, yet there is nothing into which we more easily fall than into a forgetfulness of him—especially when we enjoy peace and comfort. Indeed, prosperity not only so intoxicates many, but it can also make them proudly rise up against God. Scarcely one in a hundred of those who enjoy the good things of God in abundance keep themselves in the fear of God and live in the exercise of appropriate humility and temperance.

For this reason, we ought more carefully to note the example which is here set before us by David. He was elevated to the dignity of sovereign power, surrounded with the splendour of riches and honours. He possessed the greatest abundance of earthly good things, and yet in the midst of princely pleasures he testifies that he is mindful of God. Calling to remembrance the benefits which God had conferred upon him, David makes them ladders by which he may ascend nearer to him. By this means he not only bridles the wantonness of his flesh, but also excites himself with a greater earnestness to gratitude, and the other exercises of godliness.

⊙ Apply

How can you stop yourself from forgetting about God when things are going well for you in this life?

How can you make sure you continue to regularly thank God for all the blessings he has showered upon you?

⊙ Pray

Thank God for all the blessings and prosperity which you may be enjoying at the moment.

Ask God to help you continue trusting him and looking to him, and not to fall away because of the comforts of this life.

~ Notes and Prayers ~

_____

_____

_____

_____

_____

_____

_____

_____

_____

_____

_____

_____

_____

_____

_____

_____

_____

_____

_____

_____

Day

79

One Thing
I Ask

Psalm 27

with John Calvin

W eighing in the scales the whole power of earth and hell, David accounts it all
lighter than a feather compared to God, whose goodness so outweighs all.

Read Psalm 27

What is David's prime concern in the midst of his troubles here?

What aspects of the LORD's goodness does David focus on?

Undivided Love

In this psalm, David rehearses the desires and meditations with which he had
exercised himself in the midst of his great dangers. The thanksgivings which he
mingles with them show that it was composed after his deliverance. With what
invincible fortitude of soul this holy man was endued, that he might overcome
the most grievous assaults of his enemies. His wonderful piety shines forth in
this: that he wished to live for no other purpose than to serve God, nor could he be
turned aside from this purpose by any anxiety or trouble.

David was banished from his country, barred from his wife, bereft of his kinsfolk
and robbed of his substance. Yet he did not desire the recovery of these things so
much as he was grieved and afflicted for his banishment from God's sanctuary,
and the loss of his sacred privileges. He asked only "one thing" from the Lord. He

disregarded all other interests, displaying his intense affection for the service of God. It was more bitter for him to be an exile from the house of the Lord than to be denied access to his own house.

Greater Love

David does not complain that he was unnaturally betrayed by his father or mother in verse 10. Rather, by this comparison he magnifies the grace of God, declaring that he would ever find him ready to help him, although he might be forsaken of all others. David meant to intimate that whatever benevolence, love, zeal, attention or service might be found among people, they are far inferior to the paternal mercy with which God encircles his people.

The highest degree of love among humans is to be found in parents who love their children deeply. But God advances us higher, declaring by the prophet Isaiah that even if a mother forgot the child of her womb, he would always be mindful of us (Isaiah 49 v 15). We basely undervalue the grace of God, if our faith does not rise above all the affections of nature. For sooner shall the laws of nature be overturned a hundred times, than shall God fail his people.

⊙ Apply

Do you think of your relationship with the Lord as constantly your prime concern, as David did?

If you have ever been let down by someone in the past, meditate on the comfort of verse 10.

⊙ Pray

Ask God to give you an undivided heart to love him and "seek his face" more than anything else.

Praise God that he is your light and your salvation, your stronghold and shelter.

~ Notes and Prayers ~

Day
80

By Mercy Alone

Psalm 32

with John Calvin

The holier anyone becomes, the further they feel from perfect righteousness, and the more clearly they perceive that they can never trust in anything but the mercy of God alone.

Read Psalm 32

What is David's greatest enemy in this psalm?

What works does David have to do to earn the forgiveness of his sins?

God as Our Enemy

David teaches that our happiness consists only in the free forgiveness of sins. Nothing can be more terrible than to have God for our enemy, nor can he be gracious to us in any other way than by pardoning our transgressions. Some are so blinded with hypocrisy and pride, and some with such gross contempt of God, that they are not at all anxious about seeking forgiveness. But there isn't a single person in existence whose conscience does not accuse them at God's judgment seat. Hypocrisy shuts the eyes of multitudes, while others are so deluded by a perverse earthly security that they are touched with no feelings of divine wrath.

A Satanic Delusion

In all ages it has been a prevailing opinion that, although all are infected with sin, they are at the same time adorned with merits, which can procure for them the favour of God. This delusion of Satan is equally common among all religions and nations.

But David goes farther, declaring that the whole life of mankind is subjected to God's wrath and curse—except in so far as he promises of his own free grace to receive them into his favour. We are only blessed when we are freely reconciled to God, and counted as righteous by him. Even after we are "born again", no work which we perform can please God unless he pardons the sin which mingles with it. So the blessedness that David celebrates utterly destroys the righteousness of works.

Sharing the Good News

David, having largely and painfully experienced what a miserable thing it is to feel God's hand heavy on account of sin, exclaims that the highest and best part of a happy life consists in this: that God forgives a person's guilt, and receives them graciously into his favour. After giving thanks for pardon obtained, he invites others to fellowship with him in his happiness, showing, by his own example, the means by which this may be obtained. Indeed, we are reconciled to God upon condition that every man endeavour to make his brethren partakers of the same benefit.

⊙ Apply

How are you tempted into thinking that you could earn God's favour or forgiveness, or that what was begun by grace could be finished by works?

When did you last endeavour to make your unbelieving friends partakers of the benefit of forgiveness by mercy alone?

⊙ Pray

Praise God that he freely forgives us and covers our sin by his mercy alone.

Ask God to help you show others, by your example or in some other way, how to obtain this supreme blessing.

~ Notes and Prayers ~

Patient Faith

Psalm 40

with John Calvin

D avid, being delivered from many great dangers, extols very highly the grace of God, and his soul is filled with admiration for the patient providence of God.

Read Psalm 40

What sort of dangers do you think David was facing in this psalm?

How does he express his faith and trust in God?

Continuing Calamity

David rejoiced that he had been delivered, not only from danger, but also from present death. Some are of the opinion that this ought to be understood of sickness, but it is rather to be supposed that David here comprehends a multitude of dangers from which he had escaped. He had certainly been more than once exposed to the greatest danger—even of death—so that with good reason, he might be said to have been swallowed up in the gulf of death, and sunk in the miry clay.

All the same, it appears that his faith had still continued firm, for he ceased not to trust in God, although the long continuance of the calamity had almost exhausted his patience. He tells us not merely that he had waited, but by the repetition of the same expression he shows that he had been a long time in anxious suspense. In proportion then, as his trial was prolonged, the evidence and proof of his faith in enduring the delay with calmness of mind was so much more apparent.

Constant Courage

The meaning, in short, is that although God delayed his help, yet the heart of David did not faint, or grow weary from delay. Rather, after he had given, as it were, sufficient proof of his patience, he was at length heard.

In his example there is set before us this very useful doctrine, that although God may not forthwith appear for our help, but rather of design keep us in suspense and perplexity, yet we must not lose courage. Faith is not thoroughly tried, except by long endurance. The result, too, of which he speaks in terms of praise, ought to inspire us with increased fortitude.

God may comfort us more slowly than we desire. But when he seems to take no notice of our condition or if (so to speak) when he seems to be inactive or to sleep, this is totally different from deceit. For if we are enabled by the invincible strength and power of faith to endure, our deliverance will at length arrive.

⊘ Apply

How would you apply this psalm to some situation in your life where you wish God would answer your prayers more quickly?

Why is it so hard for us to be patient in waiting for God to act sometimes?

⊙ Pray

Praise God that he is great and good, all the time—whether he is "coming quickly ... to help us" as we would like, or not.

Ask God to give you patient faith, and not to "go astray after a lie" (v 4, ESV) while you wait for him to answer your prayers.

~ Notes and Prayers ~

Why Are You Downcast?

Psalm 42

with John Calvin

Tempted with despair, inner conflict and sorrow, the writer of this psalm strengthens his hope through prayer and meditation on the grace of God.

Read Psalm 42

What sort of conflict does this psalm tell us about?

How does the writer address it and counsel himself?

Sad to Be Separated from God

The psalm-writer preferred access to God's sanctuary to all the enjoyments, riches, pleasures and honours of this world—that in this way he might strengthen his faith and piety. It would have been less distressing to him to have been deprived of life than to continue in a state of exile from the presence of God.

The way in which we ought to regulate all our affections is this: that, on the one hand, our *joy* may have respect to the paternal love and favour of God towards us; and that, on the other, the only cause of our *grief* may arise from feeling that he is angry with us. Let us, therefore, whenever the ungodly spitefully taunt us that God is against us, never forget that it is Satan who moves them to speak in this manner, in order to overthrow our faith.

O My Soul!

The writer represents himself as if he formed two opposing parties. In the exercise of faith, he relied upon the promises of God. So he set himself, in opposition to the affections of his flesh, to restrain and subdue them. At the same time, he rebuked his own cowardice and stupidity of heart. Although he carried on war against the devil and the world, he does not enter into open and direct conflict with them. Rather, he regards *himself* as the enemy he chiefly desires to oppose.

The best way to overcome Satan is to maintain an internal conflict against the desires of our own hearts. The author's soul was cast down within him—for when our infirmities rise up in vast array, and like the waves of the sea are ready to overwhelm us, our faith seems to us to fail. We are so overcome by fear that we lack courage, and are afraid to enter into the conflict.

Whenever such a state of faint-heartedness seizes us, let us remember this: that to govern and subdue the desires of our hearts, and especially to contend against the feelings of distrust which are natural to all, is not an unusual conflict for the godly.

⊙ Apply

Why are our emotions more often linked to how things are going in this world than they are to our relationship with God?

What can you learn from the psalm-writer's example about talking to your own soul?

⊙ Pray

Praise God that a relationship with him is the most solid, real and satisfying thing in the universe.

Ask God to help you, as feelings go up and down, to keep fighting the world, the flesh and the devil.

~ Notes and Prayers ~

Day
83

Faith
and Fear

Psalm 46

with John Calvin

The faithful have no reason to be afraid, since God is always ready to deliver them—and he is armed with invincible power.

Read Psalm 46

What are the reasons to be afraid, in this psalm?

What are the reasons not to be afraid?

Keep Calm

When things are so confused that the heavens seem, as it were, to fall with great violence, the earth to shift out of its place, and the mountains to be torn up from their very foundations—we continue to maintain calmness and tranquillity of heart. It is easy to appear confident, so long as we are not placed in imminent danger. But if, in the midst of a general crash of the whole world, our minds continue undisturbed and free of trouble—this is proof that we trust God's power.

The sacred poet says, "We will not fear" (v 2). But he is not to be understood as meaning by this that the minds of the godly are exempt from all worry, as if they were destitute of feeling. For there is a great difference between indifference and the confidence of faith. It is not that the children of God, when placed in peril, indulge in joking or make light of death. But the help which God has promised them more than outweighs all the evils which inspire them with fear.

257

Be Still

The author seems at the end of the psalm to turn to the enemies of the people of God, who mischievously take revenge on them. They don't consider that in hurting the saints, they are making war against God. They imagine that they are just dealing with mere humans, and so they arrogantly assault them. The psalm-writer slaps them down, and has God say to them, "Be still".

Accordingly, the prophet rightly requires the enemies of God's people, the church, to be still and hold their peace, so that they may perceive that they are fighting against God. In short, the author exhorts the world to subdue and restrain their turbulent affections, and to yield to the God of Israel the glory which he deserves. He warns them that if they proceed to act like madmen, it will be no difficult matter for him to stretch forth his arm and glorify himself in every land. God has more than enough strength to preserve and defend his church.

⊙ Apply

What would you say to someone who said that the church was weak and powerless in this world?

When the world is in turmoil, how can being a Christian help you to "keep calm"?

⊙ Pray

Thank God that he is the defender and preserver of the church, and more than strong enough to look after his people.

Ask God to help you not to be afraid when it seems that things are going against you or against the church in general.

~ Notes and Prayers ~

Day
84

Pleasing God

Romans 8 v 5-11

with Thomas Cranmer

Those who fantasise that they are set at liberty from doing all good works and may live as they please trifle with God and deceive themselves.

Read Romans 8 v 5-11

What does Paul mean, that the mind set on the flesh cannot please God (v 8)?

Is it possible for a Christian to please God?

Living in Sin

Do not deceive yourselves, thinking that you have faith in God or that you love God or do trust in him or do fear him, when you live in sin. For then your ungodly and sinful life declares the contrary, whatever you may say or think.

It pertains to a Christian to have this true Christian faith, and to test themselves whether they have it or not, and to know what belongs to it, and how it works in them. A true faith cannot be kept secret, but when occasion is offered it will break out and show itself by good works. The soul that has a lively faith in it will always be doing some good work which shall declare that it is living, and will not be unoccupied.

Living Faith

Faith gives life to the soul, and those who lack faith are as dead to God as those who lack souls are dead to the world. Without faith, all that is done by us is but dead before God, although the work seems never so glorious before man.

Even as the picture engraved or painted is but a dead representation of the thing itself, and is without life or any manner of moving, so are the works of all unfaithful persons before God. They appear to be lively works, but truly they are but dead, not leading to eternal life. They are but shadows and shows of lively and good things, and not good and lively things indeed.

For true faith gives life to works, and out of such faith comes good works that are truly very good works; yet without it, no work is good before God. As Augustine says, we must not set good works before faith, nor think that before faith someone may do any good work. For such works, although they seem to other people to be praiseworthy, yet truly they are but vain, and not allowed before God. They are like the course of a horse that runs out of the set path, labouring hard but to no purpose.

⊙ Apply

If it is true that "without faith it is impossible to please God" (Hebrews 11 v 6), how does God view the seemingly praiseworthy works of your non-Christian friends?

Does your own life match your profession of faith, or is your faith secret and inactive?

⊙ Pray

Pray that your non-Christian friends would not be like the horse running like crazy outside the set course, but would come to have faith in Christ to animate their works.

Ask God to give you a living faith, which spills out into good works and shows itself.

~ Notes and Prayers ~

Day
85

Renew a Right Spirit within Me

Psalm 51

with John Calvin

D avid set an example to all who sin, teaching us to humbly comply with calls to repentance, instead of remaining under sin until we are surprised by the vengeance of heaven.

Read Psalm 51

Why do you think David wrote this psalm for us to read?

What does he say that God wants above all?

Thankful for Forgiveness

For a long period after his melancholy fall (after he slept with Bathsheba and had her husband killed, 2 Samuel 11), David seems to have sunk into spiritual lethargy. When roused from it by the prophet Nathan, he was filled with self-loathing and humiliation in the sight of God. He was anxious to show his repentance to all around him, and leave some lasting proof of it to posterity.

Having his eyes directed to the hatefulness of his guilt, he encourages himself to hope for pardon by considering the infinite mercy of God. This he praises in high terms, and with a variety of expressions, as one who felt that he deserved multiplied condemnation.

He prays for restoration to the favour of God. He is conscious that he deserved to have been cast off for ever, and deprived of all the gifts of the Holy Spirit. He promises, should forgiveness be granted, to retain a deep and grateful sense of it.

Hardness of Heart

We have here a striking illustration of the mercy of God in sending Nathan the prophet to reclaim David when he had wandered. By that sinful step he had placed himself at a distance from God. We do not imagine that David, during this interval, was so wholly deprived of the sense of religion as no longer to acknowledge the supremacy of the Divine Being. In all probability he continued to pray daily, engaged in the acts of divine worship, and aimed at conforming his life to the law of God.

There is no reason to think that grace was wholly extinct in his heart—but only that he was possessed by a spirit of infatuation on one particular point, and laboured under a fatal lack of awareness about his present exposure to divine wrath. Grace, whatever sparks it might emit in other directions, was smothered.

Well may we tremble to contemplate the fact that so holy a prophet and so excellent a king should have sunk into such a condition! We are indebted entirely to the grace of God, for both our new birth and any subsequent restoration.

⊘ Apply

Search your own heart: is there anything which you should confess openly to God, or which he has been calling you to repent of for some time?

Are you going through the religious motions but fatally hardened to some serious, unconfessed sin?

⊙ Pray

Confess to God that you are a sinner in need of constant forgiveness and cleansing.

Ask God to blot out your sins and give you a contrite, repentant heart, because he is a merciful and gracious God.

~ Notes and Prayers ~

Envying
the Arrogant

Psalm 73

with John Calvin

No one can form a right judgment about God's providence unless they elevate their mind above the earth and are shown the truth by God's word.

Read Psalm 73

Why does Asaph, the writer of this psalm, envy the arrogant and wicked of this world?

What made him change his mind about this?

Confusing Conclusion

Satan has numberless crafty tricks by which he dazzles our eyes and bewilders the mind. The confusion which prevails in the world produces a thick mist, which makes it difficult for us to see through it and come to the conclusion that God governs and cares for us. The ungodly, for the most part, triumph. They deliberately stir up God's anger; yet he seems to spare them—which makes it seem as if they do nothing wrong by showing him contempt, and that they will never be called to account for it.

On the other hand, the righteous groan and sigh, pinched with poverty, oppressed with many troubles, harassed by multiplied wrongs, and covered in disapproval. The more earnestly they endeavour to do good to all, the more the wicked seem to take advantage. When such is the state of things, who is not sometimes tempted by the unholy suggestion that the affairs of the world roll on at random and, as we say, are governed by chance?

Entering God's Sanctuaries

Asaph condemns himself for thinking in these ways. But he also acknowledges that he was not altogether disentangled from the doubts with which his mind had been perplexed until he entered into God's sanctuaries (v 17, the word is plural in the original).

When people are merely under the guidance of their own understandings, the inevitable consequence is that they sink under their trouble, not being able by their own deliberations and reasonings to arrive at any certain conclusions. All that deserves to be called true wisdom consists in this one point: that we submit to the teaching of the word of God.

Entering into his sanctuaries means coming to the school of God, i.e. until God becomes my schoolmaster, I understand nothing about the subject. I learn by his word what otherwise my mind cannot comprehend. We are unfit to contemplate the arrangements of divine providence until we obtain wisdom from somewhere other than ourselves. How can we attain to wisdom but by submissively receiving what God teaches us both by his word and by his Holy Spirit?

⊘ Apply

In what ways are you tempted to envy those who are not Christians?

How does knowing God's word and his plan help us to handle the confusions of this world?

⊙ Pray

Thank God that he is in total control of the world, and that he is utterly good—even when we can't quite see how that is working out in the world.

Ask God to give you wisdom from his word to help you understand this world better.

~ Notes and Prayers ~

Day
87

Overwhelmed in Despair

Psalm 88

with John Calvin

This psalm supplies the afflicted with a form of prayer, that they might not faint under any adversities, however grievous.

Read Psalm 88

Whose fault is it that the writer of this psalm feels so distressed?

Are there any signs of faith and hope in this psalm?

Praying in the Dark

This psalm contains very grievous lamentations, poured forth by its inspired writer when under very severe affliction, and almost at the point of despair. Whilst struggling with sorrow, he also declares the invincible steadfastness of his faith by calling upon God to deliver him, even when he was in the deep darkness of death. The Spirit of God, by the mouth of Heman, has here furnished us with a form of prayer for encouraging all the afflicted who are on the brink of despair to come to himself.

The Scriptures, when speaking of the providence of God, accommodate their style to the state of the world as presented to the eye. Our thoughts ascend only by slow degrees to the future and invisible world.

The psalm-writer here gives voice to some confused conceptions which arise in the mind of a man under affliction. Faith is deeply rooted in the hearts of all his genuine servants; yet sorrow often so overclouds their minds, for a time, as to take away all remembrance of his providence. From also reading the complaints of Job, we may perceive that when the minds of the godly are preoccupied with sorrow, they do not immediately pierce to the consideration of the secret providence of God.

God Who Saves Me

Such a dreadful flood did not prevent the writer from lifting up his heart and prayers to God. It was a sign of rare faith and piety to persevere as he did with never failing earnestness in prayer. We may learn from his example to cast the anchor of our faith and prayers direct into heaven, in all the perils of shipwreck to which we may be exposed. He did not call God, at the opening of the psalm, the God who saves him—and then bid farewell to all hope of comfort from him.

When the heart is in perplexity and doubt, faith seems to be swallowed up. But while it fluctuates amidst these agitations, it is nevertheless sheltered and cherished. The tempests may be violent, but it shields itself from them by reflecting that God remains faithful, and never finally disappoints or forsakes his own children.

⊙ Apply

Do you worry about emotionally expressing to God your feelings about some anguish in your life or a friend's?

What would you say to someone who said that being a Christian makes you immune from suffering and depression?

⊙ Pray

Tell God, with honest faith, how you really feel about the struggles in your life or the life of a suffering friend.

Thank God that he is "the God who saves [you]" and does not finally forsake his own children.

~ Notes and Prayers ~

Numbered Days

Psalm 90

with John Calvin

H ow wretched our condition is if we allow our hearts to rest in this world, especially when God summons us to his judgment seat.

Read Psalm 90

How does Moses, the writer of this psalm, feel about his mortality?

What things does he pray for?

Hearts Set on Eternity

Unbelievers yield themselves to indulgence in pleasures because they have their hearts set upon this world too much. They do not taste the pleasures of a celestial eternity. Why do we have such great anxiety about our life, and complain that nothing is ever good enough or sufficient, but because we foolishly imagine that we shall nestle in this world for ever? Let us learn not to be fretful and impatient, but elevate our minds, by faith, to God's heavenly throne—from which he declares that this earthly life is nothing.

Longing for Heaven

It seems absurd to pray that we may know the number of our years. Since even the strongest scarcely reach the age of eighty, is there any difficulty in reckoning up so small a sum? Children learn numbers as soon as they begin to talk, and we do not need a teacher in arithmetic to enable us to count the length of a hundred upon our fingers. So much the more shameful is our stupidity in never truly comprehending the shortness of our life. Even those who can accurately understand millions of millions are still unable to count eighty years of their own life. It is surely a monstrous thing that people can count how many feet the moon is distant from the centre of the earth and what space there is between the different planets, and yet they cannot number seventy years in their own case. It is therefore evident that Moses had good reason to ask God for this ability, which requires a wisdom that is very rare among mankind.

We truly apply our hearts to wisdom when we comprehend the shortness of human life. What can be a greater proof of madness than to ramble about without having any purpose in life? True believers alone—who know the difference between this transitory state and a blessed eternity, for which they were created—know what ought to be the aim of their life. The great purpose of mankind's existence in this world is that they may aspire after the prize of the heavenly calling.

⊙ Apply

How often do you seriously contemplate your own mortality?

Do you aspire after "the prize for which God has called [us] heavenwards" (Philippians 3 v 14), or are you locked into this world too much?

⊙ Pray

Thank God that in Christ we have an amazing future to look forward to.

Ask God to give you a greater sense of the superiority of the world to come.

~ Notes and Prayers ~

Day
89

Delighting
in God's Word

Psalm 119 v 1-16

with John Calvin

We are well fortified against the entangling nets of Satan when God's law is deeply seated in our hearts. For unless we have a fast and firm hold there, we will readily fall into sin.

Read Psalm 119 v 1-16

How many different words are used to describe God's law?

What does God's word do?

Path to Blessing

Everyone naturally aspires after happiness, but instead of searching for it in the right path, they prefer wandering up and down through endless by-ways, to their ruin and destruction. The Holy Spirit deservedly condemns this apathy and blindness. The further anyone wanders from God, the happier do they imagine themselves to be, and so all treat as a fable what the Holy Spirit declares about true piety and the service of God.

But a godly and righteous life consists in walking in the law of God. If a person follows their own will and whims, they are certain to go astray. Even if they enjoy the applause of the whole world, they will only weary themselves with vanity. The only sure protection is to regulate ourselves according to God's word.

Attracted by Sweetness

We are aware that the majority of mankind are so much involved in the cares of the world as to leave no time or leisure for meditating upon the doctrine of God. And even if we were not so ensnared by the world, we know how readily we lose sight of the law of God in the daily temptations which suddenly overtake us. It is not, therefore, without reason that the prophet exhorts us to direct our energies to the subject of constant meditation on God's precepts.

Since our lives are unstable, being continually distracted by the sinfulness of our minds, the psalm-writer declares that he will consider attentively the ways of God. Subsequently, he repeats the exquisite pleasure he took in this pursuit. For our proficiency in the law of God will be small, until we cheerfully and heartily set our minds upon it. Indeed, the beginning of a good life consists in God's law attracting us to him by its sweetness.

In the same way, the lusts of the flesh are also subdued or diminished. In our natural state, what is more agreeable to us than that which is sinful? This will be the constant tendency of our minds—unless the delight which we feel in God's law carries us in the opposite direction.

⊙ Apply

Which temptations or worldly cares are the ones which distract you most from thinking about God's word?

How can you develop a greater appetite and delight for God's word?

⊙ Pray

Thank God for his word, which brings us clarity and light to live by.

Ask God to help you hide his word in your heart, so that you will not sin against him.

~ Notes and Prayers ~

Day
90

Lift up
Your Eyes

Psalm 121

with John Calvin

T he writer of this psalm states that it is impossible to find salvation anywhere
else than in God's fatherly care, to encourage true believers confidently to
trust in his aid.

Read Psalm 121

What reasons does the psalm give to trust God?

Why might the writer struggle to trust God?

Tempted to Look Elsewhere

The thoughts of the godly are never so focused on the word of God as not to be occasionally carried away to something else that seems alluring. When dangers worry us, or when we are assaulted by painful temptations, it is almost impossible for us not to be moved by the enticements presented to us. We are so inclined to earthly things, until our minds put a restraint on themselves and are turned back to God.

We are so naturally unfaithful that, as soon as we are struck by any fear, we turn our eyes in every direction looking for help—until faith, drawing us back from all these erratic wanderings, directs us exclusively to God. We are all prone to be deceived and easily fooled. The only difference between believers and unbelievers in this respect is this—Satan bewitches unbelievers by his enchantments; but with regard to believers, God corrects the vice of their nature and does not permit them to persevere in going astray.

So the first two verses ought to be read together, thus: When I have lifted up my eyes to the mountains, then I will eventually realise that I have fallen into a rash and unprofitable mistake. Rather, I should direct them to God alone, and keep them fixed upon him.

Constant Protector

Whatever advantages worldly people are accustomed to desire or hope for from the world, true believers will find these abundantly in God alone. The psalm not only attributes power to God, but also teaches that he will preserve us in all respects in perfect safety.

As often as the power of God is extolled, there are many who immediately reply, "It is very true that he can do such and such things *if he is so inclined*, but we do not certainly know what is his intention". In this passage, therefore, God is presented to the faithful as their guardian, that they may rest with assured confidence on his providence. It is difficult for us to get rid of all anxiety and fear, but God keeps watch unceasingly over our safety.

⊙ Apply

Where else are you tempted to look for help when things are difficult, other than to God?

Is it a comfort to you that, though you are prone to wander, God is unwaveringly faithful?

⊙ Pray

Praise God for his unceasing protection, care and concern for your welfare.

Ask God to help you be faithful to him, as he is to you.

~ Notes and Prayers ~

~ Glossary ~

Apollos

Apollos was a native of Alexandria in Egypt, an eloquent man who was knowledgeable about the Scriptures and whose visit to Ephesus is recorded in Acts 18 v 24. Some Christians in Corinth counted themselves as his followers (see 1 Corinthians 1 v 12; 3 v 4) and Paul affirmed that he was a servant of the Lord (1 Corinthians 3 v 5-6).

Apostles / False apostles

The apostles were twelve men whom Jesus chose from among his disciples, and to whom he gave the name "apostles", which means an ambassador or specially commissioned messenger of the gospel, sent to proclaim it (Luke 6 v 13-16). *False apostles* (the term is used in 2 Corinthians 11 v 13) are those who pass themselves off as apostles but really are not, and who teach something other than true apostolic doctrine.

Augustine

Augustine (AD 354-430) was Bishop of Hippo in modern-day Algeria, and one of the most influential theologians of all time. The Reformers read and often quoted Augustine to show that their teaching was not novel or strange. Until he was excommunicated, Luther was an Augustinian Friar, and followed the so-called Rule of St. Augustine—a set pattern of rules for living in religious community (other types of monks followed different rules, such as the Rule of St. Benedict or St. Francis).

Blasphemy

Blasphemy is acting or speaking offensively against God, often in a dramatic or crude way (such as "taking his name in vain" as the third commandment puts it, Exodus 20 v 7, KJV).

Benedict

Benedict of Nursia (AD 480-c.545) is known as the founder of western European monasticism. His pattern of life for monks in the monasteries he founded, known as the Rule of St. Benedict, was adopted by many religious communities of monks throughout the middle ages. See also *Augustine* and *Francis*.

Blessed/cursed

To be blessed is to be approved of and praised by God and in his favour, and therefore to be fortunate, happy and well-supplied. The opposite of being blessed is being cursed: not approved of or praised by God, out of his favour, unfortunate, unhappy and deprived of good.

Circumcision

Sorry to get frighteningly medical, but circumcision is the removal of the foreskin from a penis. This was laid down as a sign of the covenant agreement between God and Abraham in Genesis 17. It was given to all Jewish boys at 8 days old as an outward sign that they were accepted as part of that covenant, and as a symbol that our sinful nature is corrupt and needs to be cut off. There were arguments in the first-century church about whether non-Jewish believers also needed to be circumcised (see Acts 15 v 1-2), and the apostle Paul (especially in Galatians) was adamant that circumcision was not necessary for salvation (see also 1 Corinthians 7 v 18-19).

Covenant

A covenant is a solemn, formal agreement which binds and defines in some way the relationship between those entering into it. In the Bible, God enters into covenant with various people including Noah, Abraham, Israel, and David—to be God to them and to their children, and to give them various things. Many, including the Reformers and some in the early church, have seen an overarching plan, a covenant of life or covenant of grace, lying behind each of these individual covenants in some way.

Covet

To covet is to want something that is not yours to have, or "evil longing and corrupt desiring" as Bullinger puts it on Day 69. It is forbidden in the tenth commandment (Exodus 20 v 17): "You shall not covet your neighbour's house. You shall not covet your neighbour's wife", etc. Since it is a sin of the mind, this shows that God is interested in more than just outward conformity to his commandments; he also cares about how we think (as Jesus also showed in Matthew 5 v 27-28).

Deity

A deity is a god or goddess. But deity can also mean "god-ness". See Colossians 2 v 9: "In Christ all the fullness of the Deity lives in bodily form".

Divine Providence

God's providence is his protective care and governance of the world. It is the opposite of chance or sheer blind luck. To trust in God's providence is to acknowledge that even when bad things seem to be happening or evil seems to prosper, God has both a plan and the power to keep his promises to us. He is in the driving seat; the journey may not always feel smooth and his route may seem mysterious, but we will get there.

Doctrine

Doctrine means teaching, or a set of beliefs about a certain subject, e.g. the *doctrine of God* is a set of teachings about God, and someone's *doctrine of justification* is what they teach about how to be right with God. It is not just a special theological term; there are well-established legal, military and political doctrines too, referring to well-known ideas, theories and policies. As Titus 1 v 9 says, an elder in the church "must hold firmly to the trustworthy message as it has been taught, so that he can encourage others by sound *doctrine* and refute those who oppose it".

Election/elected/elect

To be elect means to be chosen. So just as to elect our politicians means we choose them, the Bible also speaks of God choosing or electing a certain group of people. E.g. Deuteronomy 7 v 6: "The LORD your God has chosen you out of all the peoples on the face of the earth to be his people".

Fantastical

When we say something is "fantastic", we often simply mean it is wonderful and amazing. When Luther speaks of "fantastical spirits" he has something far less positive in mind! It means someone who is carried away by their own visions, imagination and false ideas. These are as unreal and without substance as a phantom, we might say (which comes from the same Greek and Latin words as fantastical).

Francis

Francis of Assisi (1181-1226) was a medieval preacher who founded a group of friars who lived according to the Rule of St. Francis. See above for the Rule of St. *Augustine* and the Rule of St. *Benedict*.

Godhead

God's "god-ness", his divine nature, is his Godhead. According to Christian theology, in the Godhead there are three Persons (the Father, the Son and the Holy Spirit). See also *Trinity*.

Gospel

We speak of gospel choirs (who sing religious music), and gospel truth (which is something trustworthy). But the word gospel does not mean religious or trustworthy—it means an announcement of good news. So the four Gospels (Matthew, Mark, Luke and John) proclaim *the* gospel, or message of good news about Jesus and the salvation he brings us by grace alone through faith alone. The Greek word for gospel is *evangel*, from which we get the word evangelist (someone who declares good news).

Hallow/Unhallow

We pray in the Lord's Prayer, "Our Father in heaven, *hallowed* be your name". To hallow something means to honour it and treat it as holy or special. To unhallow, therefore, is to do the opposite. See also *Holy*.

Holy

Holy means special, sacred, set apart, pure, perfect. It is the adjective used to describe God more often in the Old Testament than any other word. Indeed, he is exceedingly holy—"Holy, Holy, Holy" (Isaiah 6 v 3). God's law, the gospel, the Sabbath, Scripture and certain people can also be described as holy, because of their relationship to him. See also *Sanctification*.

Imputation/imputes/imputed

To impute something to someone is to credit or attribute it to them, to reckon it to their account. To impute righteousness to someone, for example, is to deem them righteous. If the Lord does not impute our sins to us, he does not count them as ours and we will not be punished for them. As David says, "Blessed is the one whose sin the LORD does not count against them" (Psalm 32 v 2). The Reformers were keen to stress that we are justified and counted as righteous by means of a gracious imputation (Christ's perfection is imputed to us and our sin is imputed to him). The alternative (as others taught) was that we can be declared righteous because we have righteousness *infused* into us, or because God makes us righteous first, or because we earn it or have it transferred to us in some way from those who are more righteous than us (such as the saints in heaven). See also *Justification*.

Incarnation

Incarnation means to embody in the flesh. So *the* incarnation is when God the Son took human flesh as Jesus Christ, so that he could be a mediator between God and humanity and die in our place.

Justification/justified

The doctrine of justification is "the main hinge on which religion turns" according to John Calvin (*Institutes* 3.11.1). It is the teaching about how we can be justified—that is, declared righteous or right with God and forgiven all our sins. To justify is a legal term meaning to acquit someone or declare them "not guilty", and is the opposite of condemn (see Deuteronomy 25 v 1; Romans 8 v 1). The Reformers were keen to stress that, in the Bible, "justification" does not mean to make someone righteous (as if they had to actually be righteous in life before they could be forgiven), but to *declare* that they are acquitted (even when their own lives are far from perfect). As Luther says on Day 8, when God

justifies us, we remain sinners at the same time. This happens because of *imputation* (see above), and is a one-off event rather than a process. See also *Righteousness*.

Passover

Exodus 12 tells us how, just before their exodus from slavery in Egypt, each household in Israel was to sacrifice a lamb. They were to eat it, and put some of its blood on their doorframes as a sign for God to literally "pass over" them as he brought judgment down on Egypt. In the New Testament, this is seen as a prophetic picture of the sacrifice of Christ, "the Lamb of God" (John 1 v 29). As Paul says, "Christ, our Passover lamb, has been sacrificed" (1 Corinthians 5 v 7).

Patriarchs

A patriarch is the father or ruling head of a household or tribe. In biblical and theological terms it often refers to the key Old Testament figures of Abraham, Isaac and Jacob from the book of Genesis, especially since Abraham is seen as "the father of many nations" (Genesis 17 v 4) and the father of all who have faith (Galatians 3 v 7).

Pharisees

The Pharisees were a group of Jews in the first century who often grumbled at Jesus because he associated with tax collectors and what they called "sinners" (Luke 5 v 30; 15 v 2). He in turn called them hypocrites (Luke 12 v 1), lovers of money, greedy and wicked (Luke 11 v 39). They ridiculed Jesus, and rejected the purpose of God (Luke 7 v 30), as well as neglecting justice and the love of God (Luke 11 v 42). They are portrayed as continually questioning Jesus on minor matters of fasting, ceremonial washing and Sabbath-keeping. Some later became Christians (Acts 15 v 5; Philippians 3 v 5).

Piety/pious

Piety is devotion to God, trying to be reverent, holy, dedicated to listening to and serving him, with an earnest prayerfulness and humility. "Pious" is sometimes used in a negative way, but being pious does not have to mean being hypocritical, sanctimonious or disengaged from the world—that is just a particular kind of piety, which is not recommended (see *Pharisees*)!

Precept
A precept is a command or rule designed to regulate thoughts, words or deeds. It is one of a number of words used to describe things in God's law, alongside "commands", "decrees", "statutes", etc. (see Psalm 119 v 1-8 for example).

Propitious
To be propitious is to be favourable towards someone, and not angry with them. God can be propitious towards sinful human beings because his wrath has been satisfied by the sacrifice of Christ on the cross in our place. See 1 John 2 v 2 and Romans 3 v 25: "God presented Christ as a sacrifice of atonement [literally, a *propitiation*], through the shedding of his blood—to be received by faith".

Reconciled/reconciliation
To reconcile is to bring together things which were previously separated. So Abraham might well have struggled in Genesis 22 to understand how to reconcile the promise that Isaac would be his heir with the command to sacrifice him—how to bring together those two things without there being a contradiction. Usually, however, the words are used to refer to reconciling people to one another, especially God to us and us to God. Christ came "to reconcile his Father to us" by his sacrifice on the cross in our place (as Article 2 of *The Thirty-nine Articles* puts it), but he also came to reconcile us to God, and, as a Mediator, to bring us together again. As Romans 5 v 10 says, "While we were God's enemies, we were reconciled to him through the death of his Son".

Redeemer/redeem/redemption
In modern English, to redeem something can mean to make up for its failings (e.g. the brilliance of this glossary redeems the author's terrible use of jargon in this book). Or it can mean swapping a token or voucher for an item in a shop (e.g. "I redeemed my book tokens to buy this excellent volume"). But biblically speaking, to redeem is to buy back, to liberate, a slave or captive by means of a ransom

or price. We are freed from slavery to sin (John 8 v 34), not by silver or gold but "redeemed ... with the precious blood of Christ" (1 Peter 1 v 18-19). Christ is therefore our *redeemer*, and what he has accomplished is our *redemption*.

Renunciation
To renounce something is to reject it, give it up and abandon it. For example, Jesus calls us to renunciation of self: "Whoever wants to be my disciple must deny themselves and take up their cross daily and follow me" (Luke 9 v 23).

Revelation
Revelation is the name of a book in the Bible. But it is also the process of revealing or uncovering something that was previously hidden or secret. That's why the book is called that—Jesus reveals various things to John (Revelation 1 v 1). The whole Bible is also said by the Reformers to be a revelation from God, rather than simply the words of humans reflecting on God and their experience of him.

Righteousness/righteous
To be righteous is to be in a right standing before God. This cannot be obtained through our own righteousness, our own collection of virtuous good deeds, which will always be imperfect and insufficient. The Reformers teach that we need a righteousness from somewhere else to be imputed to us, counted as ours, in order to be righteous. Since Christ lived a life of perfect righteousness and holiness, it is his righteousness that we need. Paul speaks about us being "in Christ Jesus, who has become for us wisdom from God—that is, our righteousness, holiness and redemption" (1 Corinthians 1 v 30). See also *Justification* and *Imputation*.

Sacraments
A sacrament, as defined in the sixteenth-century *Book of Common Prayer*, is "an outward and visible sign of an inward and spiritual grace given unto us, ordained by Christ himself". Roman Catholicism teaches that there are seven sacraments (baptism, confirmation, holy communion, confession, marriage, holy orders, and the anointing of the sick). The Reformers said that only two of these are really sacraments (baptism and the Lord's supper); the other five (as Article 25 of *The*

Thirty-nine Articles puts it) "being such as have grown partly of the corrupt following of the Apostles, partly are states of life allowed in the Scriptures; but yet have not like nature of Sacraments with Baptism, and the Lord's Supper, for that they have not any visible sign or ceremony ordained of God".

Saints

Saint is the word sometimes used to translate the Greek and Hebrew terms in the Bible for "holy one"or "pious, godly one". It is a biblical title given to all God's people in general, not just particularly special ones. For example, Paul's letter to the Ephesians is addressed to "God's holy people in Ephesus" (NIV), which the old King James Version translated as "the saints which are at Ephesus". (For an Old Testament example, see translations of Psalm 16 v 3.) A very long time ago, Christians began referring to particularly prominent (and usually dead) believers as Saint Augustine or Saint Anthony etc., which may be accurate in their individual cases but is not as broad as the way the Bible uses this designation. The Reformers were keen to point out that we should not worship these saints, or pray to them (but to God alone).

Salvation

Salvation means being saved or rescued from something. In the Bible, God's people are saved from Egypt, from various enemies, and ultimately from God's wrath (Romans 5 v 9). The Reformers were also keen to focus on the fact that, as Article 6 of *The Thirty-nine Articles* puts it, "Holy Scripture containeth all things necessary to salvation" (see 2 Timothy 3 v 15). Extra ceremonies or actions or teachings that others might impose were not required—we are saved by grace alone, through faith alone in Christ alone, as we discover in Scripture alone (rather than in human traditions).

Sanctification/sanctifies

To be sanctified means to be holy. The word is used in two senses: first, in a definitive, once-and-for-all sense of consecrating or setting someone apart as holy and separate; and second, in the sense of a progressive, ongoing process of becoming more holy. In 1 Corin-

thians 6 v 11 we are told about the definitive event: "You were washed, you *were sanctified*, you were justified in the name of the Lord Jesus Christ and by the Spirit of our God". And in 1 Thessalonians 4 v 3 we seem to be urged to make progress in the process of sanctification: "It is God's will that you should be *sanctified*: that you should avoid sexual immorality..." (and see 1 Peter 1 v 15-16). See also *Holy*.

Trinity

According to Christian theology, there is one God in three persons: God the Father, God the Son, and God the Holy Spirit. Each is distinct (the Father is not the Son; the Son is not the Spirit; and so on), but there is one substance or essence. As *The Thirty-nine Articles* put it, "There is but one living and true God ... And in the unity of this Godhead there be three Persons, of one substance, power, and eternity; the Father, the Son, and the Holy Ghost [Spirit]" (Article 1). This is a belief shared by Protestants, Roman Catholics and Eastern Orthodox Christians, though there have always been debates about some of the finer points of this doctrine, and over how much of it was revealed to believers in the Old Testament. See also *Godhead*.

Vainglory

Vainglory is excessive pride in one's own achievements or abilities, the sinful vanity of mankind exalting themselves over God, to whom all glory and honour and praise should go. As Paul says, "Whatever you do, do it all for the glory of God" (1 Corinthians 10 v 31).

Wittenberg

A university town on the River Elbe in eastern Germany, now known officially as Lutherstadt Wittenberg, this was Martin Luther's home and base of operations during the Reformation. In 1508, he became a professor at the relatively new university there (founded in 1502), and it was on the door of the Castle Church that he posted his famous 95 theses against indulgences on 31st October 1517. Although Luther probably only meant this as a call to have an academic debate on the subject, this event is often referred to as the start of the Protestant Reformation.

EXPLORE

BY THE BOOK

More from the series...

Allow Mark Dever and Mike McKinley to sit alongside you as you open up your Bible day by day. Their helpful questions, insightful explanations and prompts to apply God's word to your life will take you to the heart of God's word and then push it deep into your heart. Enjoy the treasures of Ruth, Jeremiah and 1 Corinthians as you explore the Bible, book by book.

Timothy Keller and Sam Allberry take you through three key New Testament sections. Experience the joy of the gospel in Romans. Wrestle with the challenging applications of James' letter. And listen to the Lord's teaching the night before he died, as recounted by John.

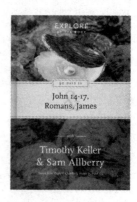

Join Timothy Keller and Richard Coekin as they lead you verse by verse through the gripping days of the judges, the gospel freedom of Galatians, and the Christ-centred glories of Ephesians.

www.thegoodbook.com/explorebythebook

EXPLORE
DAILY DEVOTIONAL

M eet the rest of the Explore family. *Explore Quarterly* is a
numbered, dated resource that works through the entire
Bible every seven years in quarterly publications, and features
contributions from trusted Bible teachers such as Sam Allberry,
Al Mohler and H.B. Charles Jr. The *Explore App* brings open-Bible
devotionals to your smartphone or tablet, enabling you to choose
between dated studies, studies on a specific book, and topical sets.

www.thegoodbook.com/explore

thegoodbook
COMPANY
Opening up the Bible

At The Good Book Company, we are dedicated to helping Christians and local churches grow. We believe that God's growth process always starts with hearing clearly what he has said to us through his timeless word—the Bible.

Ever since we opened our doors in 1991, we have been striving to produce resources that honour God in the way the Bible is used. We have grown to become an international provider of user-friendly resources to the Christian community, with believers of all backgrounds and denominations using our Bible studies, books, evangelistic resources, DVD-based courses and training events.

We want to equip ordinary Christians to live for Christ day by day, and churches to grow in their knowledge of God, their love for one another, and the effectiveness of their outreach.

Call us for a discussion of your needs or visit one of our local websites for more information on the resources and services we provide.

Your friends at The Good Book Company

UK & EUROPE   thegoodbook.co.uk   0333 123 0880
NORTH AMERICA   thegoodbook.com   866 244 2165
AUSTRALIA   thegoodbook.com.au   (02) 6100 4211
NEW ZEALAND   thegoodbook.co.nz   (+64) 3 343 2463

WWW.CHRISTIANITYEXPLORED.ORG
Our partner site is a great place for those exploring the Christian faith, with a clear explanation of the good news, powerful testimonies and answers to difficult questions.